Chronicles of Pride
A Teacher Resource Guide

Patricia Richardson Logie
Lila Burdett Kilroy
Valerie Overgaard (Editor)

Detselig Enterprises Ltd.
Calgary, Alberta

©1991 Patricia Richardson Logie

Canadian Cataloguing in Publication Data

Logie, Patricia Richardson
Chronicles of pride. A teacher resource
guide

Supplement to: Logie, Patricia Richardson.
Chronicles of pride : a journey of discovery.
ISBN 1-55059-027-8

1. Indians of North America—Canada—Study
and teaching. 2. Métis—Study and teaching.*
3. Inuit—Canada—Study and teaching.*   I.
Kilroy, Lila Burdett, 1942-   II. Overgaard,
Valerie.   III. Title.
E89.L63 Suppl.   971'.00497   C91-091317-X

Detselig Enterprises Limited
P.O. Box G 399
Calgary, Alberta T3A 2G3

Printed in Canada   SAN 115-0324   ISBN 1-55059-027-8

About the Authors

Patricia Richardson Logie

For the last eight years, Patricia Richardson Logie, the artist of the paintings called *Chronicles of Pride*, has been dedicated to this project. She has toured throughout British Columbia with the thirty-one portraits and has written a book about the people who make up *Chronicles of Pride.* Her experiences have also lead to the production of a video to accompany the paintings and the book. Her goal is to celebrate the contributions of First Nations peoples and their cultures, and to educate people about those contributions.

Patricia Richardson Logie has been an established portrait painter for the last thirty years. She studied at Sir John Cass College in London, exhibited with the Royal Society of Portrait Painters, the Pastel Society, and was invited to join the Society of Women Artists. Patricia has taught for the Federation of Canadian Artists and the University of British Columbia. Her paintings are included in the Vancouver School Board Collections, and in many private collections across Canada, in the United States, Japan, and England.

Lila Burdett Kilroy

Lila Burdett Kilroy began working in Native Indian education over twenty years ago in the public school system in Merritt, British Columbia. Many of her first students were relatives from the Shulus Reserve. Lila has lived with and taught First Nations peoples in British Columbia and in Saskatchewan. Her experience spans preschool to adult education and includes teaching in public schools and in schools on reserves. Lila is currently working for the Vancouver School Board in the Inner City Schools Project.

Lila completed a Bachelor of Education at the University of Victoria, and a Master of Education in Education Administration at the University of British Columbia. She is currently a doctoral candidate in Curriculum and Instruction at Brigham Young University in Utah.

Valerie Overgaard

Valerie Overgaard has held several positions in the area of curriculum, including Research Coordinator for the Curriculum Branch of the British Columbia Ministry of Education, Senior Researcher and Writer for the Royal Commission on Education in British Columbia, and Curriculum Development Specialist for the Vancouver School Board. She is the author of several educational publications, among them *A Handbook for Curriculum Development*. Valerie has produced curriculum resource guides on Vancouver's Chinatown, on the University of British Columbia's Museum of Anthropology, and has participated in the production of several others. She is currently the Academic Assistant to the Dean of Education at the University of British Columbia.

Valerie Overgaard graduated from the University of British Columbia with a Bachelor of Education and taught in the public school system in British Columbia and Alberta. She subsequently became involved in human rights issues working as an education coordinator in the labor movement in Alberta. She completed a Master of Arts in Curriculum and Adult Education at the University of Victoria. She is presently completing her doctoral studies in Curriculum Theory at Simon Fraser University in Burnaby.

Contents

Section VI

Keeping Traditions Alive

Section VII

Section VIII

Living Off The Land:
Activities and Information about Traditional Ways

Acknowledgments

Without help and encouragement, supportive funding, professional involvement, dedication, and a strong mutual belief in the philosophy of the project, the work for this guide could not have been accomplished. Fortunately for the program, the right person or the right association appeared at the right time, and we would like to thank them all.

Secretary of State/Multiculturalism

United Church, British Columbia Conference

The Professional Native Women's Association:
Gloria Nicholson, Executive Director

The Vancouver School Board:
Native Advisory Committee
Dr. John Wormsbecker, past Deputy Superintendent
Lorna Williams, Native Indian Education Consultant
Betty Wellburn, District Principal Visual Arts

Native Indian Teacher Education Program, University of British Columbia:
Jo-Ann Archibald, Program Supervisor
Mandy Jimmie, Student
Beatrice Silver, Student

The Vancouver Museum:
Donna Bryman, Education Coordinator

Judith Filtness

Fran H. Eger

Ken Haycock

Introduction

Background

Peoples who were living in North America for many thousands of years, long before the Europeans arrived on these shores, are called aboriginal or indigenous. Today, the Canadian constitution recognizes three major groups of aboriginals: the Inuit (Eskimo), the Indians,[1] and the Métis (descendents from mixed marriages).

Each major group of aboriginal peoples is made up of different nations and each nation has a different language, a different culture, different beliefs, and different ways of life. Each group has its origin in a particular geographical area. It is impossible, then, to study Native peoples as though they are one group. However, while there are differences in many aspects of their cultures which should be recognized, there are also similarities among the First peoples of this country.

Prior to contact with the Europeans, Native peoples had a relationship with the land based on respect and understanding for the ecosystem. Their cultures and ways of life were influenced by the environment. They had great respect for Nature, for all things animate and inanimate. Their traditions and histories were recorded in people's memories through dance, songs, stories and legends, some of which have now been recorded in writing. Contact with white people changed many of their ways of life.

The descendants of the First peoples have learned about traditional ways of life through their ancestors. Many draw energy from the spirituality of their cultures. They have, in many cases, preserved and revived their languages, their art and their customs. Their dynamic cultures are gaining strength in their own traditions and power in the Canadian political arena. Today, Native

---

1   This guide uses several different terms to refer generically to the indigenous or aboriginal peoples of Canada. "Indian" is a term officially used by government and in government documents. "First Nations " is a term preferred by most people when referring generically to the indigenous peoples of Canada; individual Nations are used to identify an individual and his or her origin. "Native", "aboriginal", and "indigenous" peoples are terms used most often by anthropologists or ethnographers. This guide uses the terms somewhat interchangeably with the understanding that these terms convey the respect intended; by using various alternatives, it is hoped that no one will be offended.

peoples are artists, farmers, actors, teachers, doctors, secretaries, politicians, fishermen, lawyers, pilots, counselors; in short, they work in and make contributions to the commercial, intellectual, spiritual, and social community. At the same time, they maintain distinct cultures.

The people portrayed in the set of paintings called *Chronicles of Pride* are a selection of the First peoples of this country. Collectively, the lives of the subjects tell a story of dignity, strength, courage, hard work and great spiritual strength. Studying some brief details of these lives will help students understand the contributions individuals make to their immediate communities and to the greater community in which they live and work. Learning about some traditional and contemporary aspects of each person's culture will help students understand why Native peoples have great pride in their heritage. These studies will also promote an understanding of some contemporary issues with which First peoples and other Canadians are concerned.

Aim and Rationale

The major aim of this resource guide is to provide educators with a vehicle for conveying, through art, the spirituality and quiet dignity of First Nations peoples and the wealth of human resources existing within their cultures. It is also the intent of *Chronicles of Pride,* by focusing on contemporary people making contributions in all aspects of society, to encourage greater understanding and communication among peoples.

In many cases, First Nations peoples are studied as cultures from the past. There is little information available in materials developed for use in schools that considers the vibrant nature of their cultures. By learning about contemporary people, students will have an opportunity to recognize the ongoing contributions, and the dynamic character of the First Nations.

Program Goals

Through the study of the individuals portrayed in the series of paintings called *Chronicles of Pride*, and discussions of the contributions of those individuals to the fabric of Canadian life, students will develop:

Knowledge and Understanding of

- the valuable contributions of Native peoples

- some aspects of First Nations cultures

- educational issues

- issues of Native rights and land claims

- portraiture as an art form

- some career opportunities

- the importance of setting goals

Abilities in

- communication

- research

- inquiry, problem solving, decision making

Attitudes of

- self-esteem

- respect for self and others

Using This Guide

This guide is meant to accompany the text *Chronicles of Pride: A Journey of Discovery*, written by Patricia Richardson Logie and published by Detselig Enterprises of Calgary, 1990, and the poster reproductions of the thirty-one portraits. It is intended that teachers will select for study a number of the individuals portrayed in the paintings and from the activities suggested, plan a unit which could be part of a *social studies*, *language arts*, *fine arts* or an *integrated* curriculum.

The activities suggested vary in their focus and in their difficulty. Some may be more appropriate for younger students, and others for older students. With a total of thirty-one portraits, there is a vast range for planning potential units of study.

For each portrait, there is a very brief section of background information provided. This includes information about the individual in the portrait, as well as some aspect of his or her culture. Any number of these portraits may be selected for study. A set of four or five might be planned as a unit.

Activities are not identified by curriculum area nor by the age group for which the activities are appropriate. It is intended that teachers in individual classrooms will use the material flexibly, based on their own students and the time available for the study. A section of *Maps* is included at the end of the guide. There are also additional print and audio visual resources suggested in the *Additional Resources* section.

It is suggested that teachers choose one portrait at a time for study. The appropriate poster may be displayed in the classroom in a frame so that it is viewed as a valuable piece of art. The person in the portrait could then be studied using the information provided in this guide, in the book and in other resource materials.

Ideally, a teacher and teacher-librarian would work together to assemble the materials students could use to research issues which are raised. The *Additional Resources* listed in the back of the guide are intended to assist in this task.

Planning a Unit of Study

Organizing Activities

The activities in the guide are organized around seven major sections.

• Section I, **Introductory Study Activities**, provides suggestions for ways to introduce a study on *Chronicles of Pride*. The activities in this section set the stage, or present an overall context for the study.

• The First Nations people who make up *Chronicles of Pride* are organized into five different sections, each representing the people's interests and accomplishments:

> Section II, **Visual and Performing Arts**

> Section III, **Education**

> Section IV, **People Helping People**

> Section V, **First Nations Rights, Politics and the Law**

> Section VI, **Keeping Traditions Alive**

Each of these sections begins with a set of learning objectives. A study of any one of the persons portrayed in the section supports the objectives named. The activities for each of the persons in the section are organized into: activities that have knowledge, understanding and abilities as their major focus, activities that encourage discussion of social issues and have values and attitudes as their focus; and activities that deal with the portraits and other examples of aesthetic expression.

• Section VII is called **Additional Activities**. The activities in this section are meant to be culminating projects — they draw on the information studied in the earlier sections and provide a way to bring closure to the study.

• Section VIII is a collection of **Additional Resources** teachers may use in planning and presenting units of study.

Selecting Activities

It is important to spend some time looking at the entire range of possibilities in order to make decisions about which people from *Chronicles of Pride* a teacher or the students would wish to study. Planning a unit can be seen as a five step process:

1. The first step in preparing a unit would be to select appropriate activities from Section I. These would introduce students to the notion of culture, to First Nations cultures in particular, to the geography and diversity of First Nations cultures in Canada, and to the individuals who are to be studied.

2. The next step would be to decide what objectives would be appropriate for the students to pursue. It may be that you would like to focus on the area of Native Rights, Politics and Law, in which case you would likely choose all the people from this section. On the other hand, you could choose one person from each of the five sections, thereby giving some attention to each of the areas of objectives. Or, you may want to choose two or three areas for study and select people from those sections. The point is that studying four to six of the people portrayed in the study can be as focused or as general as you wish in terms of the areas of objectives to be pursued.

3. Having chosen the areas of objectives and the people who are included in those sections, the next step is to actually decide on a selection of activities for students to engage in. These would likely be a balance of activities which focus on knowledge, understanding and abilities, attitudes and aesthetic expression.

4. Then, a project, or set of activities from **Additional Activities** should be chosen to wrap up or extend the study.

5. The activities chosen will likely call upon the use of a number of resources: print, audio visual and human. These should be organized by checking the **Resources** section and cooperating with the school's teacher-librarian.

The following outlines, one for elementary students and one for secondary students, are offered as examples of how a teacher might select a variety of subjects and activities that would comprise a unit of study.

The following outlines are meant to provide samples of units a teacher may want to develop from the materials in this guide. They are not meant to represent the best examples, but are included for the sake of illustration. The activities listed here are found in later sections of this guide.

Sample Unit Plan for Elementary Students

Introduction to Unit

(from Introductory Study Activities, pp. 18-20)

Discuss the cultural background of students in your class. On a world map, locate the place of origin of each student's ancestors. Discuss the notion of immigration. Introduce the terms "indigenous" and "aboriginal".

Invite a Native storyteller to the classroom to share stories with the students or have students listen to the recording *Native Storytelling* (see *Additional Resources*, p. 119). Have students prepare questions for the guest.

Have students draw pictures to illustrate the stories they were told by the story teller. Ask them to talk about their pictures to the rest of the class.

Help students understand what "culture" means and how a culture is represented in people's customs and traditions (food, dress, language, beliefs, celebrations, art, music, dance, etc.). Discuss customs of students in the classroom. Make a chart to compare and contrast customs. Discuss some of the customs of First Nations peoples. Ask students to look for similarities and differences between these customs and their own. Help students understand that we are all similar in many ways. It is our differences that make us unique, and this diversity is to be valued.

Introduce vocabulary students may find useful: *aboriginal, indigenous, culture, diversity, First Nations, reserve, band, achievements, issues, spiritual, contributions, self-esteem, pride, dignity.* Have them use some of the words in stories or illustrate them in pictures.

On a map of the province or of the country, have students show the geographical location of each Native Indian Nation (see *Maps* section). Ask students to write down the name of each nation: e.g., Kwakiutl, Micmac, Cree. Discuss the idea of diversity. Discuss the use of various names or labels used to refer to aboriginal peoples (see Note on p. 1 explaining the use of various names to refer to Canada's First peoples).

Show the video *Chronicles of Pride* (see *Additional Resources*, p. 115) and discuss the project undertaken by Patricia Richardson Logie. Discuss the possible reasons for doing a project like this. Ask students to consider what the value of the project might be. Explain to students that the subjects in the paintings have made valuable contributions to the lives of other people and that they will be finding out about these people in the study they are about to begin.

First Subject Study: Education

Verna Kirkness: (from Suggested Study Activities, p. 37)

Introduce Verna Kirkness by telling the students something about her background and discussing her accomplishments. In addition to the brief information provided in this guide, more details can be found in the book, *Chronicles of Pride: A Journey of Discovery* (see *Additional Resources,* p. 106).

The painting of Verna Kirkness is quite different from others in the series. The artist was portraying her own perceptions of the subject. Discuss the artist's perception of Verna Kirkness.

Native people believe strongly in having control over the education of their children. It is through education that the young will learn about their own culture and heritage and will be able to build their own beliefs. Discuss the importance of education for passing on tradition and the consequences of being denied that right.

Education does not only take place in institutions such as schools. In Native cultures, the elders are the teachers of the traditional ways. Show the films *Kevin Alex* and *Our Totem is the Raven* (see

Additional Resources, p. 116, 117) which depict young Natives learning about their traditional ways. Ask students write or tell stories about important things they have learned in places other than school.

Show the film *Cold Journey* (see *Additional Resources*, p. 115) which tells the story of a young Native boy who faces the cruelty of a white man's school and searches for meaning in his life. Discuss the importance of education which respects the value of Native culture.

Verna Kirkness remembers being keen to go to school as a child. Ask students to imagine how difficult it would have been to attain the education Verna has. Discuss what qualities would be needed to accomplish what Verna has achieved. Ask students to write a story about Verna as a young girl.

Second Subject Study: Visual and Performing Arts

Daphne Odjig: (from Suggested Study Activities, p. 22)

Introduce Daphne Odjig by telling the students something about her background and discussing her accomplishments. In addition to the brief information provided in this guide, more details can be found in the book, *Chronicles of Pride: A Journey of Discovery* (see *Additional Resources*, p. 106).

Ask students to compare and contrast the environments in which coast peoples and Ojibway live. Ask them to find out how peoples in each geographical area made use of their environments. Have them consider how this may have influenced their art (e.g., color, line, form, etc.).

Discuss what qualities would be needed to accomplish what Daphne has achieved. Have students consider how others might develop those qualities. Ask them to write a story of their future picturing themselves as successful adults and describing how they achieved their success.

Show the film *The Colours of Pride* (see *Additional Resources*, p. 116) about the work of Daphne Odjig and other Woodland artists. Discuss the film. Ask students to write a story or poem about their favorite painting.

Collect examples or pictures of Native art. Ask students to compare styles of the various Nations' art: line, color, form, materials, etc. Have them find out the purpose or function of some of the art (e.g., to record history, to express personal relationships, to denote status, for decoration, for gifts). Exhibit the art in the school hallway.

Third Subject Study: Visual and Performing Arts

Walter Harris: (from Suggested Study Activities, p. 32)

Introduce Walter Harris by having students ask questions about his portrait. In addition to the brief information provided in this guide, more details can be found in the book, *Chronicles of Pride: A Journey of Discovery* (see *Additional Resources*, p. 106). Any questions that can't be answered could become part of the study.

While students are studying the painting, ask them to consider why Patricia Richardson Logie chose the size canvas she did. Ask students to suggest what the effect would have been had the artist used a different shape of canvas.

Northwest Coast Native cultures (see *Maps* sections) are known for their carvings of totem poles. Ask students to find out about the different types of poles that were carved or different purposes for which poles were carved (e.g., house poles, mortuary poles). Ask them to find out about the art of other Native cultures in Canada and to choose one to study.

Show the film *Totem Poles* (see *Additional Resources*, p. 118) which shows seven different kinds of Northwest Coast poles. Ask students to consider the technology used for carving in traditional times and technology which is available today.

The work of Walter Harris is displayed in many places in the world. Discuss the sense of accomplishment and pride Walter Harris must feel. Have students write letters to Walter Harris, expressing their thoughts about his work and his success. (Send to Band Office, Kispiox, B.C., V0J 2J0).

Help students carve a totem pole (or make one using clay, plasticine, papier mache or other material). This could be an individual or a class project, depending on the size of the pole being carved. Have students write and perform a short play about the pole they made.

Invite a Native artist to class to discuss Native art forms and their meanings, or visit the studio of an artist in your area.

Fourth Subject Study: Keeping Traditions Alive

David Gladstone: (from Suggested Study Activities, p. 83)

Introduce David Gladstone by telling students he is a young man who has made it his goal to preserve the traditions of his people. Discuss his reasons for doing this. In addition to the brief information provided in this guide, more details can be found in the book, *Chronicles of Pride: A Journey of Discovery* (See *Additional Resources*, p. 106). Show the film *The Great Spirit* (see *Additional Resources*, p. 116), which demonstrates that many Native peoples are gaining strength from their traditional ways. Discuss this idea.

Teach children some Native songs and discuss their significance. For example, use the publication and tape "People of the Salmon" (see *Additional Resources*, p. 119) available from the Vancouver School Board, 1595 W 10th Avenue, Vancouver, B.C., V6J 1Z8.

Wearing traditional costumes and dancing the ritual dances are rights which must be earned in the Heiltsuk culture. Ask students to find out what one must do to "earn the right" to wear the traditional costumes and perform the songs and dances.

Songs and dances are important parts of all Native ceremonies and each has special significance. Play some Native songs. Have students draw pictures to illustrate the images the songs evoke. Watch some Native dance, if possible, and discuss its importance in the ceremonies of the people.

Have students consider the painting of David Gladstone. Ask them what the background in this painting might mean (i.e., the doorway from the old to the new). Have students compare David's dress to that of Simon Baker and Leonard George.

Summary for Unit

(from Additional Study Activities, pp. 89-92)

Have students develop their own *Chronicles of Pride* using themselves and family members. Focus on each individual's accomplishments, endeavors and dreams. Pictures and photographs could be used. Students should recognize all accomplishments, great and small.

Sample Unit Plan for Secondary Students

Introduction to Unit

(from Introductory Study Activities, p. 18-20)

Discuss the cultural background of students in your class. On a world map, locate the place of origin of each student's ancestors. Discuss the notion of immigration. Introduce the terms "indigenous" and "aboriginal".

On a map of the province or of the country, have students show the geographical location of each Native Indian Nation (see *Maps* section). Ask students to write down the name of each nation: e.g., Kwakiutl, Micmac, Cree. Discuss the idea of diversity. Discuss the use of various names or labels used to refer to aboriginal peoples (see Note on p. 1 explaining the use of various names to refer to Canada's First peoples).

Collect newspaper articles which note some achievements of Native people or issues concerning them. Ask students to organize the collection according to important themes. Have them choose one issue or person to investigate further.

Show the video *Chronicles of Pride* (see *Additional Resources*, p. 115) and discuss the project undertaken by Patricia Richardson Logie. Discuss the possible reasons for doing a project like this. Ask students to consider what the value of the project might be. Explain to students that the subjects in the paintings have made valuable contributions to the lives of other people and that they will be finding out about these people in the study they are about to begin.

First Subject Study: Native Rights, Politics and Law

A Tribute to a Unique Moment in History: (from Suggested Study Activities, p. 73)

Introduce James Gosnell, Joe Mathias, and Bill Wilson by showing the film *Dancing Around the Table* (see *Additional Resources*, p. 116) which depicts the Native involvement in the Constitutional debate. Ask students to take a role from the film and to reenact the scenario from their own understanding of the issues. Ask students to find out about the debates that followed over the "Meech Lake Accord". Ask them to consider the role Elijah Harper played in defeating the Accord. Discuss the issues in the debate about the Constitution.

James Gosnell said, regarding the Constitutional questions, "I want my grandchildren to be able to read in history that when they patriated the Constitution and our rights were being discussed, that we were there representing our people to make the fight on behalf of title." Other Native peoples thought they should boycott the event, not even get involved. Discuss this issue. Ask students which position they think was right and why.

In a speech to a symposium on Aboriginal Title held in Victoria in 1983, Bill Wilson said, "The only concept of title that really means anything to me ... and to other Native Indian people across the country is the feeling inside ourselves about our relationship with the land...." Ask students to explain what they think he means by that statement. Read the quote from Chief Seattle (p. 82) and ask students to relate the two ideas.

Collect newspaper articles which discuss issues of Native rights. Have students discuss the issues and conduct debates about the positions taken.

Invite a local Native politician to class. Have students prepare questions for discussion about some political issues (e.g., aboriginal rights, land claims).

Discuss the composition and background of the painting and the statement made by the artist.

Second Subject Study: Native Rights, Politics and Law

Mildred Gottfriedson: (from Suggested Study Activities, p. 76)

Introduce Mildred Gottfriedson by telling the students something about her background and discussing her accomplishments. In addition to the brief information provided in this guide, more details can be found in the book, *Chronicles of Pride: A Journey of Discovery* (see *Additional Resources*, p. 106).

Show the film *Somewhere Between* (see *Additional Resources*, p. 118) which outlines the controversy surrounding laws which discriminate against Native women. Have students discuss the feelings expressed by the women in the film.

Section 12(1) of the *Indian Act*, until it was amended in 1985, meant that women who married non-Indians would lose their status as Indians. On the other hand, women who were non-Indian but married Indian men were granted status. Discuss the policy and consider its purpose. Have students explore the early history of government decisions involving Native women's rights.

Mildred Gottfriedson accomplished much in her life. Ask students to consider the qualities a person needs to succeed. Discuss the importance of setting goals and how personal expectations can lead to personal achievements and can affect individuals or groups. Have students set a personal goal for the next month and after the month is up have students discuss their successes.

Discuss the painting of Mildred Gottfriedson. Consider why the artist selected the pose, colors, background, etc.

Third Subject Study: Education

Robert Sterling: (from Suggested Study Activities, p. 43)

Consider the painting of Robert Sterling. Have students think about why the artist painted the subject this way. Ask them to suggest what statement the artist is making.

Education has long been considered an important aspect of all cultures. Discuss the importance of education for individuals and for cultures. Ask students to write stories or reports which indicate the importance of education.

Native people believe strongly in having control over the education of their children. It is through education that the young will learn about their own culture and heritage, and will be able to build their own beliefs. Discuss the importance of education for passing on tradition and the consequences of being denied that right. Get a copy of the Native position paper on education (see *Additional Resources*, Native Indian Brotherhood, p. 112) and discuss the issues.

Many of the subjects of the portraits in *Chronicles of Pride* are educators or are primarily interested in the role of education. Some have worked as politicians to improve conditions for their people. Discuss the different view points of educators and politicians and the role each can play in furthering the rights of First Nations peoples. Have students write and present a speech from the point of view of:
• an educator
• a politician.

Guujaaw: (from Suggested Study Activities, p. 81)

Ask students to study the painting of Guujaaw. Introduce Guujaaw by having students ask questions that arise from viewing the picture. After providing students with information based on their questions, have them describe how the painting relates to what they know about the man. In addition to the brief information provided in this guide, more details can be found in the book, *Chronicles of Pride: A Journey of Discovery* (see *Additional Resources*, p. 106).

Discuss why Gary Edenshaw prefers to be known by his Haida name, Guujaaw. Have them investigate the importance of naming in Native cultures.

Chief Seattle, in 1852, said

> ...This we know. The earth does not belong to man: man belongs to the earth. This we know. All things are connected like the blood which unites one family. All things are connected. Whatever befalls the earth befalls the sons of the earth. Man did not weave the web of life, he is merely a strand in it. Whatever he does to the web, he does to himself...

This statement reflects the beliefs of many First Nations peoples. Discuss what it means. Ask students to suggest why environmental concerns would arise from these beliefs. Ask students to choose an environmental issue to research and relate the issue to the interconnectedness of all things. Show the film *I Was Born Here* (see *Additional Resources*, p. 116), a tribute to the intense relationship between Native peoples and the land.

Guujaaw lives by the beliefs of his ancestors. He wishes to preserve a life that respects and understands the complex relationships in the ecosystem. Ask students to write letters to environmental groups to find out what beliefs they hold, and have students compare these with Guujaaw's.

Fifth Subject Study: Keeping the Traditions Alive

Agnes Alfred: (from Suggested Study Activities, p. 85)

Show the film *Potlatch: A Strict Law Bids Us Dance* (see *Additional Resources*, p. 117). Agnes Alfred is one of the people in the film which recreates the supposed "last potlatch" in 1922. Discuss the importance of the potlatch to Northwest Coast Native cultures. Ask students to imagine they were living in 1884 when the government ban was declared. Have them write letters to the government to express their opinions about the tradition of the potlatch.

Using the British Columbia Teachers' Federation Lesson Aid #2011 *To Potlatch or Not to Potlatch* (see *Additional Resources*, p. 113), distribute articles to groups of students. Have them take one of the positions (a government official recommending the banning of the potlatch, Chief Maquinna appealing to the government to lift the ban, etc.) and debate the issues as presented.

Discuss what wealth meant to traditional Native people. Ask students to compare this with what wealth means to the average North American today.

Contact a local band council and try to arrange a class visit to their reserve. Have students prepare questions for the elders. Tape record and photograph the elders if allowed.

Ask students to express how they feel about the painting of Agnes Alfred. Ask them to consider in their appraisal: color, composition, brush strokes, statement, etc.

Sixth Subject Study: Keeping Traditions Alive

A Promise: (from Suggested Study Activities, p. 87)

Discuss the painting "A Promise". Ask students to suggest why the artist chose that title. Focus discussion on what students think are the attributes that promote a feeling of promise; what they see in the eyes of the subjects; what they believe these young people could be when they mature; and what they believe Native children could accomplish that would help their people. Discuss why Native children are considered a first natural resource.

Education does not only take place in institutions such as schools. In Native cultures, the elders are the teachers of the traditional ways. Show the films *Kevin Alex* and *Our Totem is the Raven* (see

Additional Resources, p. 116, 117) which depict young Natives learning about their traditional ways. Have students write or tell stories about important things they have learned in places other than school.

Summary for Unit

(from Additional Study Activities, p. 89-92)

Have students write a speech as if they were one of the subjects in the portraits. The speech could be on personal achievements, leadership traits, or tribal group. Speeches could be tape recorded or videotaped.

Introductory Study Activities

The activities listed in this section are meant to provide a general introduction to the study of *Chronicles of Pride.* By engaging in a number of these activities, students will have an opportunity to learn about the First Nations peoples and will be prepared to study individual subjects in this context.

Culture, First Nations Culture

Discuss the cultural background of students in your class. On a world map, locate the place of origin of each student's ancestors. Discuss the concept of immigration. Introduce the terms "indigenous" and "aboriginal".

Invite a Native storyteller to the classroom to share stories with the students or have students listen to the recording *Native Storytelling* (see *Additional Resources*, p. 119). Have students prepare questions for guest.

Have students draw pictures to illustrate the stories they were told by the story teller. Ask them to talk about their pictures to the rest of the class.

Have students research their personal and family history. Ask them to create a family tree or learn a story from one of their older relatives who can remember times past. Ask students to share their stories or family trees with each other.

Help students define "culture" and understand how a culture is represented in people's customs and traditions (food, dress, language, beliefs, celebrations, art, music, dance, etc.). Discuss customs of students in the classroom. Make a chart to compare and contrast customs. Discuss some of the customs of First Nations peoples. Ask students to look for similarities and differences between these customs and their own. Help students understand that we are all similar in many ways. It is our differences that make us unique, and this diversity is to be valued.

Introduce vocabulary students may find useful: *aboriginal, indigenous, culture, diversity, First Nations, reserve, band, achievements, issues, spiritual, contributions, self-esteem, pride, dignity*. Discuss their meanings. Have students use some of the words in stories or illustrate them in pictures.

Collect newspaper articles which note some achievements of Native people or issues concerning them. Ask students to organize the collection according to important themes. Have them choose one issue or person to research.

Geography, Diversity

On a map of the province or of the country, have students show the geographical location of each Native Indian Nation (see *Maps* section). Ask students to write down the name of each nation: e.g., Kwakiutl, Micmac, Cree. Discuss the idea of diversity. Discuss the use of various names or labels used to refer to aboriginal peoples (see Note on p. 1 explaining the use of various names to refer to Canada's First people).

On a map of Canada, have students record the major Native language groups (see *Maps* section). Discuss the diversity represented.

On a map of Canada have students mark the birthplaces and/or work areas of the people in the *Chronicles of Pride* series. Have students write the name of the person and his or her tribe or nation on the map.

Individuals In **Chronicles of Pride**

Show the video *Chronicles of Pride* (see *Additional Resources, p. 115)* and discuss the project undertaken by Patricia Richardson Logie. Discuss the possible reasons someone would want to do a project like this. Ask students to consider what the value of the project might be. Explain to students that the subjects in the paintings have made valuable contributions to the lives of other people and that they will be finding out about these people in the study they are about to begin.

Have students choose one person from the *Chronicles of Pride* series as "the person of the month". Display the subject's picture and biography. Discuss why that person was chosen, relate some biographical information about the person, and ask students to comment on the statement made in the painting. In addition to the brief information provided in this guide, more details can be found in the book *Chronicles of Pride: A Journey of Discovery* (see *Additional Resources*, p. 106).

In each case as well, it would be appropriate for the teacher to introduce biographical and geographical information on the portrait subjects in a variety of ways:

- question and answer

- interview situations (radio or T.V. simulation)

- role play in groups (e.g., carry on a conversation as if several of the subjects were together discussing a topic).

When reviewing a given portrait in the series, have students brainstorm about what they think that person is doing now. Ask them to suggest why the artist may have chosen the person.

Conduct a discussion about the actual painting — color, tone, light, perspective, composition, brush strokes, statement, etc.

Section II

Visual and Performing Arts
Daphne Odjig
Lyle Wilson
Margo Kane
Dorothy Francis
Leonard George
Walter Harris

Section Objectives

By studying the individuals portrayed in this section and engaging in the activities suggested, students will develop:

The Knowledge and Understanding

- that Native artists, working in various mediums, contribute to Canada's artistic community

- that First Nations peoples have distinct artistic styles that are recognized and valued worldwide.

- that the traditional art and dance of First Nations peoples complement the stories that are part of their oral culture, and to some extent, record the history of First Nations peoples.

Abilities in

- communication

- research

- inquiry, problem solving, decision making

Attitudes of

- self-esteem

- respect for self and others

Painting #1 *Chronicles of Pride* Series
Size: 30 x 42 (76.2 cm x 106.68 cm)

Daphne Odjig

Artist, Honorary Doctorate of Laws,
Order of Canada

Daphne Odjig was born in 1919 at Wikwemikong Reserve, Manitoulin Island, Ontario. She is of the Odawa tribe, Ojibway Nation.

Daphne is a renowned artist, highly respected in this country and internationally. One of her best known works is a mural called *The Indian in Transition*. It was commissioned by the Canadian Museum of Civilization (the National Museum of Man) and is exhibited in the National Arts Centre in Ottawa. The mural, eight feet by twenty-seven feet, is an impressive work of art. Daphne's paintings from her exhibition "Time Passages" are in the background of the portrait.

Cree and Ojibway art, often referred to as "Woodlands art", is unique in its color and form. Daphne, along with such well-known artists as Norval Morrisseau, have been key in reviving and extending this art form and in making it internationally known. Daphne has been an inspiration to her people. Among her awards are an Honorary Doctorate from the University of Toronto for her art and the Order of Canada for her artistic contribution to her country.

Suggested Study Activities: (Daphne Odjig)

Knowledge, Understanding, and Abilities

Have students research the method used by universities to select individuals who are awarded Honorary Doctorates. Have them research the accomplishments of one or more people who have received Honorary Doctorates.

Ask students to compare and contrast the environments in which coast peoples and Ojibway live. Ask them to find out how peoples in each geographical area made use of their environments. Have them consider how this may have influenced their art (e.g., color, line, form).

Discuss the idea of being in transition. Discuss how in some ways the students are in transition, and how as individuals and as part of a group, we are always in transition. Have students write an essay entitled "The Indian in Transition". Ask them to focus on developing a better understanding of and respect for Native people. As preparation for this activity, students should read some literature about contemporary and past First Nations cultures. They may also contact the National Arts Centre in Ottawa requesting further information on the painting.

Have students make a mural. Ask them to choose a subject that portrays some aspect of First Nations culture. Have students discuss the statement they want to make and create a plan to put it all together. Have them choose a director to help unify the concepts. When the mural is complete, have students present it, along with a commentary, to the other students in the school.

Attitudes

Discuss the qualities needed to accomplish what Daphne has achieved. Have students consider how others might develop those qualities. Ask them to write a story of their future picturing themselves as successful adults and describing how they achieved their success.

Aesthetic Expression

Show the film *The Colours of Pride* (see *Additional Resources*, p. 116) about the work of Daphne Odjig and other Woodland artists. Discuss the film. Ask students to write a story or poem about their favorite painting.

Ask students to comment on the paintings in the background of the portrait (Odjig's exhibition, "Time Passages"). Have them think about how the paintings are different from or the same as other art work with which they are familiar.

Collect examples or pictures of Native art. Ask students to compare styles of the various Nations' art: line, color, form, materials, etc. Have them find out the purpose or function of some of the art (e.g., to record history, to express personal relationships, to denote status, for decoration, for gifts). Exhibit the art in the school hallway.

Take students to a gallery where Native art is sold. Have them prepare questions for the gallery staff: Who are the artists?, Who buys the art?, etc.

Painting #2 *Chronicles of Pride* Series
Size: 24 x 30 (60.96 cm x 76.2 cm)

Lyle Wilson
Artist

Lyle Wilson comes from Kitimat, British Columbia. He was born at Butedale Cannery in 1955. Lyle is a member of the Haisla-Kwakiutl language group.

It is interesting to note that Lyle's birth place is a cannery. Many First Nations peoples from the Interior of British Columbia travel during the fishing season to work in the canneries. Whole families move into the cannery and establish a temporary "village" in the company housing. The adults work shifts in the plant while the older children look after the younger ones.

Lyle is an artist who works in silver. He is also adept at other forms of art such as etching, lithography, graphics, and engraving. In his art work, he incorporates contemporary concepts into the traditional Northwest Coast style. Lyle studied at Emily Carr School of Art in Vancouver and majored in art during his teacher training at the University of British Columbia. He has done work for the University of British Columbia Museum of Anthropology, recreating the traditional art of his people.

Suggested Study Activities: (Lyle Wilson)

Knowledge, Understanding, and Abilities

Lyle's birth at a cannery is one consequence of living in accord with seasonal changes. Ask students to first speculate about possible consequences of each season's character. Make a chart to indicate the characteristics of the season (weather, availability of animal and plant life for food, etc.) and record students' ideas about the consequences. Then ask them to find out if their speculations were correct by referring to library resources.

Native art often portrays different animals in symbolic style. Discuss the cultural significance and symbolism of animals. Using information from the *Wisdom of the Elders* (see *Additional Resources*,

Kirk, p. 111), explain to students that animals represented family crests and identified the lineage of the family. Read legends about Raven, Bear, Eagle, Thunderbird, Coyote, etc. Have students write and illustrate their own legends.

Attitudes

Lyle is a teacher and an artist. Ask students to interview the teachers in their school to see if any of them have an outside interest such as art, and why they chose teaching as a career.

Aesthetic Expression

Visit a museum of anthropology. Have students study the silver carvings on display and discuss the shapes and the forms used. Ask students to look for the same forms in artwork using other materials (e.g., wood carvings, argillite carvings, paintings).

Invite a Native artist to class to discuss Native art forms and their meanings, or take students to an artist's studio or school of art to observe him or her at work.

Provide students with opportunities to do some traditional art: beadwork, jewelry, carving, button blankets, weaving, etc.

Consider the composition and color in the painting of Lyle Wilson. Discuss what statements the painting makes about the subject and his people (e.g., strength, quietness, dignity).

Painting #4 *Chronicles of Pride* Series
Size: 24 x 28 (60.96 cm x 71.12 cm)

Margo Kane

Actress

Margo Kane is of Cree descent. She was born near Edmonton, Alberta in 1952.

When she was nineteen, Margo decided to take up a career in acting and dance. She is now successful as an actress, a singer, and a dancer, having worked in theatre, on television, and in movies. Because of her interest in theatre and her support of the culture, Margo dreams of a great Canadian Native Indian production.

Margo was raised by "non-Indians" but chose to identify with the spiritual nature of the Native people. She draws strength from her traditional background, and has worked with many young Native students to inspire them.

She was chosen to play the role of Rita Joe in the play *The Ecstasy of Rita Joe,* and in researching the role, she became aware of the many problems young Natives face. She has spent a great deal of time since then speaking to young people, encouraging them to set goals for themselves and to be proud of their accomplishments.

Suggested Study Activities: (Margo Kane)

Knowledge, Understanding, and Abilities

Have students find out if there is a program for Native youth in your area. (For example, a Native Youth Program is sponsored by the University of British Columbia Museum of Anthropology). If so, invite a member of the group to visit the class to speak about the program. Ask students to make oral reports about their findings.

Contact one of the Fellowship Centres or Native organizations in your area (consult your telephone directory). Invite someone from the centre or organization to speak to the students about any programs they have for young people. Have students prepare questions for the speaker.

Attitudes

Ask students to research the story of Rita Joe (see *Additional Resources*, Ryga, p. 112). Ask them to consider why being involved in the play might have inspired Margo Kane to work with Native young people. Have students take the roles of the characters in the play and perform some scenes from it.

Margo Kane is a role model to many young people. Discuss what a role model is. Ask the students to write about their own role models and to explain why they chose them.

Aesthetic Expression

Patricia Richardson Logie says she painted Margo Kane "as if she were in the spotlight: caught up in the emotion of the moment." Discuss what this may mean. Ask students what emotion was captured in the painting. Have them do a self-portrait or a portrait of a classmate. Show an "emotion of the moment".

Have students study the painting of Margo Kane. Ask them to consider what the colors in the background of the portrait suggest to them.

Have students attend a dramatic, music or dance performance, or invite performers to the class. Discuss the skills, effort and dedication involved in such an event.

Drama has always played an important role in culture. Discuss what roles drama plays in the students' culture. Ask students to consider why that may be so. Invite a theatre group to the school to perform a play.

Painting #5 *Chronicles of Pride* Series
Size: 24 x 28 (60.96 cm x 71.12 cm)

Dorothy Francis
Order of Canada

Dorothy Francis is Salteaux, born on the Waywayseecappo Reserve in Manitoba. Her name in Salteaux is *Maqua Beak*, meaning bear.

Dorothy Francis has promoted her culture through work in radio (singing and reading poetry), television (telling children stories), and live performances and demonstrations (crafts, storytelling, dance, and song). She was a key person in founding Native Friendship Centres. For her efforts in keeping her culture alive, she was awarded the Order of Canada.

The picture of Dorothy shows her in the traditional dress of the Plains Indian, a beaded buckskin. Her spirituality is depicted through two important symbols: the bear and sweetgrass. The bear is a symbol of strength, loyalty, and nurturing. The sweetgrass is a prairie plant that is burned in ceremonies — in spiritual ceremonies, prayers are thought to rise with the smoke. The smoke of the sweetgrass purifies and cleanses those who are touched by it.

Suggested Study Activities: (Dorothy Francis)

Knowledge, Understanding, and Abilities

There are several individuals in the series *Chronicles of Pride* who have received the Order of Canada. Have students research the method used by the federal government to select individuals who are awarded the Order of Canada. Ask students to investigate the accomplishments of other people who have received the Order of Canada.

Dorothy Francis used the media to share her traditions. Discuss the use of media to promote culture. Have students focus on the purpose and impact of promoting culture through the various forms of media.

Storytelling is important to all Native cultures. Play the cassette *Native Storytelling* (see *Additional Resources*, p. 119). Have students illustrate or dramatize the stories. Discuss the importance of storytelling to Native cultures.

Attitudes

Dorothy Francis' name in Salteaux is *Maqua Beak*, meaning bear. Names are very important to Native peoples and are given to them in ceremonies. Ask students to discuss their own names: how they were given, if they have been changed, what they mean to them and to their families. Discuss the differences in the ways cultures think about names. Ask students to think about how they would feel if someone told them they had to change their name.

The bear in the Salteaux culture is a symbol of strength and loyalty. Ask students to choose some other animals and to find out what they symbolize. Have them report on their findings. Ask each student to select an animal symbol that suits him or her. Ask them to explain their choices.

Aesthetic Expression

Discuss the painting of Dorothy Francis. Ask students to note the light around the subject's head and consider what it might mean. Ask students to list words which describe the feeling they have when they look at the painting. Make a chart of all the suggestions and ask students to use the words to write a poem or a song.

In the portrait, Dorothy Francis wears a buckskin, the traditional dress of Plains people. Have students note the beadwork. Have them find out about beading and what materials Native peoples used before they had glass beads from European traders (e.g., quills, shells, seeds). Ask them to find out about the designs used by various cultural groups.

Have students research the traditional dress of other Native peoples. Students could make cutout dolls dressed in traditional clothing of various cultures, including ceremonial costumes.

Painting #14 *Chronicles of Pride* Series
Size: 24 x 36 (60.96 cm x 91.44 cm)

Leonard George

Singer, Dancer, Film Producer

Leonard George is a member of the Coastal Salish, Burrard Band, Burrard Reserve, North Vancouver, British Columbia. He was born in 1946.

Dance and song are important aspects of Leonard George's culture. Individuals in his culture have dances which are their own and which they can pass down through their families; other dances are rituals for important events. Leonard George performs traditional dances at ceremonies and for visiting dignitaries. He speaks of the drumbeat as the heartbeat of mother earth and of the spiritual force that moves his people to sing and dance. He is an actor, film maker, and producer.

At one time, Leonard George had to battle alcoholism. He now speaks to young people about these problems and encourages them to devote their time to better things. He is the founder of the Dan George Memorial Foundation which is named after his father and is intended to promote the development of Native people in the field of television, film, and video.

Leonard George wears an eagle feather in his portrait, a symbol of strength and a reminder to people that we are all part of nature, and as such, are relatives of the birds in the sky. He believes that when he wears the eagle feather he must walk tall. Patricia Richardson Logie has painted Leonard in the traditional Coast Salish costume that he wears when he dances.

Suggested Study Activities: (Leonard George)

Knowledge, Understanding, and Abilities

Leonard George talks about the eagle feather, symbolism and personal dignity. Discuss the importance of the feather (and other forms of symbolism). Ask students to paint or draw symbols from other cultures in a way which expresses what the symbols represent.

Through his work in the entertainment field, Leonard George is communicating a strong message about his culture. Discuss this concept. If possible, watch some traditional Native dances and find out about their significance.

Read the legend *Little Badger and the Fire Spirit* (see *Additional Resources*, Campbell, p. 104). Discuss the theme of drumbeats as the heartbeat of the universe. As an art project, make drums and have students create their own dances. (*Thanks to Charlotte Pierre, Vancouver School Board, for suggesting this activity*.)

Leonard George was instrumental in founding the Dan George Memorial Foundation, located in Vancouver, British Columbia. Dan George, Leonard's father, was also from the Burrard band. He was born in 1899 and died in 1981. He was a logger, longshoreman, construction worker, and musician. He is known for his acting (*Little Big Man* with Dustin Hoffman), for his work on stage (*Ecstasy of Rita Joe*), and his writing (author of *My Heart Soars*, and *My Spirit Soars*). Discuss Dan George's accomplishments and ask students to speculate about the purpose of the foundation.

Attitudes

Leonard George says he must walk tall when he wears the eagle feather. Ask students to suggest things that make them feel like "walking tall". Have them draw pictures of themselves in a situation where they would walk tall. Have them literally walk tall while they describe to other students what it feels like.

Aesthetic Expression

In the portrait, Leonard George wears the eagle feather. Discuss what effect this has on the portrait's impact. Have students consider the composition of the painting, the meaning of the symbol, and the relationship of the two.

Teach children some Native songs and discuss their significance. For example, use the publication and tape *People of the Salmon* (see *Additional Resources*, p. 119) available from the Vancouver School Board, 1595 W 10th Avenue, Vancouver, B.C., V6J 1Z8.

Play the recording *The Drums of Poundmaker* (see *Additional Resources*, p. 118). Ask students to draw the images which come to their minds when they hear the sound of the drums.

Show the film *Journey to Strength* (see *Additional Resources*, p. 116). Discuss the production. Have students write film reviews about it.

Painting #24 *Chronicles of Pride* Series
Size: 18 x 40 (45.72 cm x 101.6 cm)

Walter Harris

Artist, Pole Carver

Walter Harris is an hereditary chief of the Kispiox, Gitksan of the Kildu. He was born in Kispiox, British Columbia in 1931.

Walter Harris is a well-known artist whose poles have been placed as far afield as San Francisco, California; Baltimore, Maryland; and Rochester, New York. Examples of his carvings can be seen over the doors in the House of Commons in Ottawa. His portrait shows him in front of his family totem pole in his village, Kispiox, on the Skeena River.

Walter Harris helped to build the village of K'san near Hazelton, British Columbia. The village is a replica of a traditional village and has examples of both pre-contact and post-contact buildings. It includes a school where various traditional arts — carving, jewelry, weaving, etc. — are taught. Students come to the school from all over the province. Walter Harris teaches students to carve masks and make totem poles and rattles.

Suggested Study Activities: (Walter Harris)

Knowledge, Understanding, and Abilities

Northwest Coast Native cultures are known for their carvings of totem poles. Ask students to research the different types of poles that were carved or different purposes for which poles were carved (e.g., house poles, mortuary poles). Ask them to study art of another Native culture in Canada .

Show the film *Totem Poles* (see *Additional Resources*, p. 118) which shows seven different kinds of Northwest Coast poles. Ask students to consider the technology used for carving in traditional times and technology which is available today.

Show the film *Bill Reid* (see *Additional Resources*, p. 115) which shows the artist carving a pole and the ceremony of raising it. Ask students to consider the importance of the raising of the pole at Skidegate on the Queen Charlotte Islands.

Visit a local museum to see totem poles. Ask students to research how poles are made and how they are erected (use materials from the *Additional Resources* section)

Attitudes

The work of Walter Harris is displayed in many places in the world. Ask students to consider the sense of accomplishment and pride the artist must feel. Have students write to Walter Harris, expressing their thoughts about his work and his success. (Send to Band Office, Kispiox, B.C., V0J 2J0).

Aesthetic Expression

Have students carve a totem pole (or make one using clay, plasticine, papier mache or other material). This could be an individual or a class project, depending on the size of the pole being carved. Have them write and perform a short play about the pole they made.

Ask students to make a model or diorama of a traditional Native village. Several groups in the class could make models of villages from different Native cultures.

Invite a Native artist to class to discuss Native art forms and their meanings, or visit the studio of an artist in your area.

Provide students with opportunities to do some traditional art: beadwork, jewelry, carving, button blankets, weaving, etc.

While students are studying the painting, ask them to consider why Patricia Richardson Logie chose the size canvas she did. Ask students to suggest what the effect would have been had the artist used a different shape of canvas.

Education
Yvonne Dunlop
Verna Kirkness
Peggy Shannon
Brenda Taylor
Robert Sterling

Section Objectives

By studying the individuals portrayed in this section and engaging in the activities suggested, students will develop:

The Knowledge and Understanding

- that education is a way all cultures introduce children to the customs of the people. If, through the education system, Native children only see the culture and customs of the non-Native population, they will be robbed of their rights to know about their own heritage.

- that the First Nations peoples of Canada have had to fight for the right to educate their own children.

- that through the education system all people can learn more about each other.

Abilities in

- communication

- research

- inquiry, problem solving, decision making

Attitudes of

- self-esteem

- respect for self and others

Painting #3 *Chronicles of Pride* Series
Size: 16 x 20 (40.64 cm x 50.8 cm)

Yvonne Dunlop
Educator

Yvonne was born in 1950 in Vancouver, British Columbia and is a descendant of the L'ilawat band at Mount Currie, Interior Salish.

Yvonne graduated from the Native Indian Teacher Education Program (NITEP) at the University of British Columbia. She taught for two years at Bella Bella, then worked with Urban Images, an organization sponsored by the Professional Native Women's Program in Vancouver. She is now a counselor/coordinator for NITEP.

Yvonne embraces the traditional beliefs of her people. She speaks of the Sacred Circle (sometimes called the Medicine Wheel) and the importance of colors in her culture. The sacred circle is a symbol which represents the interrelatedness of all things. It represents an holistic system of organization — there is no beginning or end. The circle reflects the natural world, the cycle of birth, life, and death; the sky, the sun and moon; the cycle of days and seasons. It represents the wholeness of a person — spiritual, emotional, mental, and physical. First peoples sit in a circle for ceremonies and meetings. The Sacred Circle is a symbol of harmony and balance: living in harmony with all aspects of Nature is a very important value.

The colors are situated around the circle — in the North is black, in the East is red, in the South is yellow, and in the West is white. These colors are also symbolic. Among other things, they represent the different peoples of the world and their different perspectives on the world.

Suggested Study Activities: (Yvonne Dunlop)

Knowledge, Understanding, and Abilities

Yvonne Dunlop has referred to several books on cultural values, traditions, and concepts: *Seven Arrows*, *The World's Rim*, *Warriors of the Rainbow*, *Voices of the Earth and Sky*, and *Great Upon a Mountain*. Ask students to choose one or more of these books for study. Discuss the symbolism of the circle, the colors, or other symbolism illustrated in the books.

Introduce the ideas of the sacred circle and the sacred tree by reading *The Sacred Tree* (see *Additional Resources*, p. 114). Ask students to draw a circle and make up symbols to represent the various parts of the circle.

Aspects of the culture of the Interior Salish are somewhat different from the coastal Nations. Ask students to consider why there are differences and what these differences are. Have them make charts to record the differences.

Attitudes

People's beliefs determine their actions in many cases. Discuss how belief in the interrelatedness of all things, living and nonliving, would affect the way people interact with their environments. Ask students to speculate about, for instance, why many First Nations peoples are active environmentalists. (Refer to Chief Seattle quote p. 82)

Yvonne Dunlop sees the education of the whole person as very important: that is, the spiritual, emotional, mental, and physical aspects of the person are all considered important. Ask students whether this approach is taken in most schools. Ask them to write short essays explaining why they think schools should (or should not) focus on all aspects of the person.

Aesthetic Expression

Invite a story teller to class to tell the students traditional stories. Discuss the beliefs the stories illustrate. Ask students to dramatize one of the stories they heard.

Patricia Richardson Logie painted two pictures of Yvonne. In the second picture which is not part of this series, Yvonne is wearing a "copper". Ask students to research "coppers" of the Northwest Coast. Have them find out what they are, what their significance is, why they are not as common as they once were, and how they have been a source of controversy for the people of the Northwest Coast.

In the picture of Yvonne, Patricia Richardson Logie has used vivid color. Discuss what colors mean to the students and how colors make them feel. Ask them to find out about the colors of the sacred circle. Ask students to write poems about a color, expressing what the color means to them.

Painting #15 *Chronicles of Pride* Series
Size: 20 x 24 (50.8 cm x 60.96 cm)

Verna Kirkness

*Director of First Nations House of Learning,
University of British Columbia*

Verna Kirkness is Cree and was born on the Fisher River Reserve in Manitoba in 1935.

Verna is a dedicated educator for whom education has always been the essence of life — both as a student and throughout her career as a teacher in Manitoba and British Columbia. In recognition of her work, the Adult Learning Centre in Winnipeg was named after her. Verna has a clear vision of the importance of bringing people together. She believes that First Nations peoples must understand themselves and that this understanding will ultimately benefit all Canadians.

Professor Verna Kirkness was the Director of the Native Indian Teacher Education Program (NITEP) at the University of British Columbia. NITEP is a program which encourages Native students to pursue careers in the teaching profession. Verna is now the Director of the First Nations House of Learning at the University of British Columbia. The primary goals of this organization are to see more Native students in all faculties, to develop relevant course content, to develop Native leadership on campus, and to encourage original research. Verna says that rather than having a Native Studies program, it is important for all faculties of the university to take First Nations values and lifestyles into account. She and her staff are working to make changes which will meet the needs of First Nations students and encourage them to pursue professions in medicine, law, education, engineering, commerce, etc.

Suggested Study Activities: (Verna Kirkness)

Knowledge, Understanding, and Abilities

Education has long been considered an important aspect of all cultures. Discuss the importance of education for individuals and for cultures. Ask students to write stories or reports which indicate the importance of education.

Native people believe strongly in having control over the education of their children. It is through education that the young will learn about their own culture and heritage, and will be able to build their own beliefs. Discuss the importance of education for passing on tradition and the consequences of being denied that right. Get a copy of the Native position paper on education (see *Additional Resources*, Native Indian Brotherhood, p. 112) and discuss the issues.

Education does not only take place in institutions such as schools. In Native cultures, the elders are the teachers of the traditional ways. Show the films *Kevin Alex* and *Our Totem is the Raven* (see *Additional Resources*, p. 116, 117) which depicts young Natives learning about their traditional ways. Ask students to write or tell stories about important things they have learned in places other than school.

Have students write to the University of British Columbia to find out about the First Nations House of Learning.

First Nations House of Learning
6365 Biological Sciences Rd.
University of British Columbia
Vancouver, B.C., V6T 1W5

Ask them to use the information to write reports or make oral reports to other students in the school.

Attitudes

Show the film *Cold Journey* (see *Additional Resources*, p. 115) which tells the story of a young Native boy who faces the cruelty of a white man's school and searches for meaning in his life. Discuss the importance of education which respects the value of Native culture.

Verna Kirkness remembers being keen to go to school as a child. Ask students to imagine how difficult it would have been to attain the education Verna has. Discuss what qualities would be needed to achieve what Verna has achieved. Ask students to write a story about Verna as a young girl.

Aesthetic Expression

The painting of Verna Kirkness is quite different from others in the series. The artist was portraying her own perceptions of the subject. Discuss the artist's perception of Verna Kirkness.

Painting #18 *Chronicles of Pride* Series
Size: 18 x 24 (45.72 cm x 60.96 cm)

Peggy Shannon
Teacher, Master of Education

Peggy Shannon is Haida and comes from Masset on the Queen Charlotte Islands of British Columbia. She was born in 1943.

As a child, Peggy Shannon attended residential school and felt robbed of her identity and feelings of self-worth. By the age of thirty-five, she was a mother and a grandmother. She decided she wanted to complete her education, and this became her goal. She started by upgrading her secondary education, went on to complete her education degree in NITEP (the Native Indian Teacher Education Program) at the University of British Columbia, and finally surpassed her original goal by obtaining her Master's degree in Education.

Peggy Shannon rose above much adversity to achieve her success, including fighting alcoholism in her background. Her accomplishments are an inspiration. She intends to raise awareness of the positive contributions of contemporary Native peoples, and to help others by working to better the lives of Native peoples.

Suggested Study Activities: (Peggy Shannon)

Knowledge, Understanding, and Abilities

Discuss the fact that at one time Native children were forced to go to missionary schools and residential schools where they were forbidden to speak their own language. (If possible, watch the CBC production called "Where the Spirit Lives".) Ask students to imagine how this restriction made the children feel. Have them write letters from the point of view of a Native child in a residential school.

Peggy Shannon is a mother and a grandmother. As a Haida she is also part of a clan. All the members of a clan can trace their heritage to a legendary ancestor. Each clan has a crest which signifies its origin and membership in the clan, and has certain privileges, songs, dances, and stories. Have students research clans (see *Additional Resources*, Kirk, *Wisdom of Elders*, p. 111).

Attitudes

Peggy Shannon was a mother, housewife, and grandmother when she decided to return to school. She received a Bachelor's degree, then a Master's degree. This is a remarkable accomplishment. Discuss how such remarkable things can be accomplished, ways of overcoming obstacles and achieving goals, and the belief that it is "never too late".

Discuss the importance of setting goals and how personal expectations can lead to personal achievements and can affect individuals or groups. Have students choose someone they know whom they think has accomplished much. Ask them to interview the person and to report their findings to the class.

Discuss the students' achievements. Have them make graphs showing their achievements. Encourage them to set goals for themselves and as they achieve a goal to mark it on their graphs. Students should be allowed to keep their graphs private if they wish.

Aesthetic Expression

Have students study the painting of Peggy Shannon and suggest what the artist was trying to say about the subject. Have them look at composition, color, brush stroke, and background of the painting to help them understand the statement the artist intended.

Painting # 27 *Chronicles of Pride* Series
Size: 14 x 24 (35.56 cm x 60.96 cm)

Brenda Taylor

Promoter of Native Education, Home/School Worker

Brenda Taylor is Kwakiutl from Bella Bella, a reserve on a small island off the coast of British Columbia. She was born in 1938.

Brenda Taylor is a Native Home/School Worker for the Vancouver School Board. In that role, she is able to advance her favorite cause — the education of Native peoples. She also devotes her time to other valuable programs and works tirelessly for what she believes in. She has been a counselor for the Boarding Home Program of Bella Bella and the Boarding Home Program Indian Education Resources Centre in the Lower Mainland. The Native Indian Youth Advisory Society was initiated by Brenda. She was also a founder of the Native Youth Program of the University of British Columbia Museum of Anthropology.

Patricia Richardson Logie describes Brenda Taylor as bright, dynamic and fun-loving with a mind as big as her heart. The artist has painted her to indicate just that.

Suggested Study Activities: (Brenda Taylor)

Knowledge, Understanding, and Abilities

Many of the subjects of the portraits in *Chronicles of Pride* are educators or are primarily interested in the role of education. Senator Len Marchand (see *Study*, p. 71) has worked as a politician to improve conditions for his people. Educators and politicians believe they can change the world in different ways: educators by reaching the young, politicians by changing the laws. Discuss the different view points of educators and politicians and the role each can play in furthering the rights of First Nations peoples. Have students write and present a speech from the point of view of:
- an educator
- a politician.

Education has long been considered an important aspect of all cultures. Discuss the importance of education for individuals and for cultures. Ask students to write stories or reports which indicate the importance of education.

Have students write to the Vancouver School Board (1595 W 10th Avenue, Vancouver, B.C., V6J 1Z8) to find out about the role of Native Indian Home-School Workers and Native Indian Cultural Enrichment Workers. Ask students to find out what other school boards do to meet the same needs.

Have students write to a school for Native students (contact a local Native organization for school locations) to ask for a pen-pal with whom they can exchange information about education and culture.

Have students find out if there is a program for Native youth in your area. (For example, a Native Youth Program is sponsored by the University of British Columbia Museum of Anthropology). If so, invite a member of the group to visit the class to speak about the program. Ask students to make oral reports about their findings.

Attitudes

Students in Bella Bella who wished to pursue their secondary education often had to move to the lower mainland of British Columbia to do so. It was for students in this situation that Brenda Taylor worked in the Boarding Home Program of Bella Bella. Ask students to think about what it would feel like to move from a small town to an urban centre in order to pursue their education. Have them write letters home from this perspective.

Show the film *Cold Journey* (see *Additional Resources*, p. 115) which follows the journey of a young Native boy as he searches for meaning in his life and experiences the cruelty of education in a white man's school. Discuss why it is important to learn about and feel proud of our own heritage.

Aesthetic Expression

Patricia Richardson Logie says she painted Brenda Taylor in a way which showed the person inside. Ask students to suggest the subject's qualities as expressed in the painting (e.g., dynamic, fun-loving, intelligent, big-hearted).

Painting #29 *Chronicles of Pride* Series
Size: 24 x 34 (60.96 cm x 86.36 cm)

Tribute to Robert Sterling

Inspirational Educator

Robert Sterling was of the Thompson Indian Nation, Lower Nicola Valley Band at Merritt, British Columbia. He was born in 1937.

Robert Sterling was an educator of outstanding ability. He instigated the Native Indian Home-School Coordinator program in British Columbia. He was also instrumental in developing the Native Indian Teacher Education Program (NITEP) at the University of British Columbia. He headed the Nicola Valley Indian Education Administration in Merritt and led with remarkable insight and dedication.

All who knew him mourned the tragic death of Robert Sterling and his son, in a canoe accident on the Thompson River in 1983. Prior to his untimely passing, he had agreed to sit for a portrait for the *Chronicles of Pride* series. Patricia Richardson Logie chose to paint a tribute to the man.

Suggested Study Activities: (Tribute to Robert Sterling)

Knowledge, Understanding, and Abilities

Education has long been considered an important aspect of all cultures. Discuss the importance of education for individuals and for cultures. Ask students to write stories or reports which indicate the importance of education.

Native people believe strongly in having control over the education of their children. It is through education that the young will learn about their own culture and heritage, and will be able to build their own beliefs. Discuss the importance of education for passing on tradition and the consequences of being denied that right. Get a copy of the Native position paper on education (see *Additional Resources*, Native Indian Brotherhood, p. 112) and discuss the issues.

Education does not only take place in institutions such as schools. In Native cultures, the elders are the teachers of the traditional ways. Show the films *Kevin Alex* and *Our Totem is the Raven* (see

Additional Resources, p. 116, 117) which depicts young Natives learning about their traditional ways. Ask students write or tell stories about important things they have learned in places other than school.

Many of the subjects of the portraits in *Chronicles of Pride* are educators or are primarily interested in the role of education. Some have worked as politicians to improve conditions for their people. Educators and politicians believe they can change the world in different ways: educators by reaching the young, politicians by changing the laws. Discuss the different view points of educators and politicians and the role each can play in furthering the rights of First Nations peoples. Have them write and present a speech from the point of view of:
- an educator
- a politician

Ask students to research Native Indian teacher education programs. Have them write to the nearest university for this information and prepare reports using the information.

Attitudes

Robert Sterling dedicated much of his life to the education of his people. Have students consider his accomplishments and the esteem in which he is held. Have students discuss how they would describe Robert Sterling and then ask them to write a "Tribute to Robert Sterling" to accompany the painting.

Aesthetic Expression

Ask students to consider the painting of Robert Sterling and why the artist painted the subject this way. Ask them what statement the artist is making.

People Helping People
John Williams
Glen Newman
Simon Baker
Vivian Wilson
Paul Willie
Blanche Macdonald
Matthew Hill

Section Objectives

By studying the individuals portrayed in this section and engaging in the activities suggested, students will develop:

The Knowledge and Understanding

- that many First Nations people are dedicated to enhancing the quality of life for their people and therefore for Canadians in general.

- that people often choose and use their professional roles to better the lives of other people.

- that by helping others, First Nations people earn respect inside and outside their communities.

Abilities in

- communication, research

- inquiry, problem solving, decision making

Attitudes of

- self-esteem

- respect for self and others

Painting #8 *Chronicles of Pride* Series
Size 24 x 30 (60.96 cm x 76.2 cm)

John Williams
United Church Minister

John Williams is Haida from the Queen Charlotte Islands of British Columbia. He was born in 1921.

John Williams, at the age of fifty-four, was ordained as a minister by the United Church of Canada. He ministered in Kitamaat for many years and has now retired to the Queen Charlotte Islands. John has also been a commercial fisherman.

As a young man, John Williams contracted tuberculosis. This is a disease which has plagued Native peoples for many years and is still a source of trouble in some areas. John was extremely ill and was not expected to recover. At one point, John thought he was about to die, and then he had a dream: John stood on the shore and saw his grandfather coming for him in his canoe, a tiny speck on the horizon. He ran to get his father's gun, but on the way back to the shore realized he had no ammunition. John called out to his cousin to tell his grandfather that he could not go with him this time. The sky was beautiful — pure indigo at the horizon, shading to pale blue, purple to mauve, then red to gold. (*Story permission of John Williams, reprinted from* Chronicles of Pride *by Patricia Richardson Logie.*)

When he awoke, John knew that he would not die. The Haida believe that when it is time for them to leave the earth, their ancestors come for them in canoes and accompany them on their journey. John realized when he woke that it was not yet time to take that journey.

Suggested Study Activities:(John Williams)

Knowledge, Understanding, and Abilities

John Williams' dream is depicted in the portrait. The dream has a great deal of significance in his culture. Discuss the dream and its significance. Ask students to find legends or stories which describe other similar beliefs. Make a chart with students to compare the different beliefs illustrated in the legends, myths, and stories of selected cultures (e.g., Ancient Greek, First Nations, Christian, Buddhist, Sikh, Jewish, Taoist).

When Europeans came to Canada, they brought with them many diseases. Among them were influenza, smallpox, and tuberculosis. Because they had not developed any resistance to the diseases, many First Nations people died from them. Smallpox itself killed more than eighty percent of some Northwest Coast Nations. Ask students to research the population of Native peoples at contact, after contact, and today (Canadian Department of Indian and Northern Affairs, Ottawa will have more information). Have them put the information on a graph and explain the reasons for the changes.

Attitudes

John Williams says he doesn't believe in preaching, but rather, thinks his role is to "leave gems that make one think and to find one's own answers". This is very characteristic of Haida culture (as well as cultures of other First Nations). Discuss this philosophy and ask students to consider the value of this belief. Ask them to find legends which illustrate the philosophy.

Aesthetic Expression

In the portrait of John Williams, the artist has made an interesting use of color, especially around John Williams' head. Ask students to note the use of color and to suggest what effect it produces. Have students comment on the dream scene that is included in the portrait.

Have students dramatize John Williams' dream. Help them make masks to use for the dramatization.

Ask students to draw pictures of dreams they have had. Ask them to tell the story of their dream to others in the classroom.

Painting #9 *Chronicles of Pride* Series
Size: 20 x 24 (50.8 cm x 60.96 cm)

Glen Newman

Band Councilor and Social Worker

Glen Newman is Squamish, born in North Vancouver, British Columbia in 1944.

Glen Newman has served in many positions in the Squamish Tribal Council. He has been a social worker, a Native consultant for the Ministry of Human Resources, and a Squamish Band Councilor and Administrator.

Band government is directed by the *Indian Act* of Canada. The *Act* establishes that there is to be an elected council and an elected chief to look after the administration of the band. The election must take place every two years and is based on popular vote. This type of government structure is not part of the traditional tribal system of governing people of First Nations, but was rather a European scheme assigned to them when the Government of Canada was given exclusive law-making authority. In traditional tribal ways, the leader achieved his position by gaining the respect and confidence of his peers, or by heredity.

Patricia Richardson Logie says Glen Newman's love and concern for people make him an outstanding humanist. She has attempted through his expression and the use of the paint and brush work around his head and shoulders, to make the viewer aware of Newman's personality.

Suggested Study Activities: (Glen Newman)

Knowledge, Understanding, and Abilities

The *Indian Act* is said by some to deny Indian Bands the right of self-government because it allows the Government of Canada extreme authority. Ask students to research the *Indian Act* and to be prepared to state their opinion on how it should (or should not) be changed.

Native peoples identify themselves with a band, a tribe, and a nation. Using maps of the area where the students live, ask students to determine the numbers and names of the bands, tribes, and nations represented in that area.

Ask students to find out how chiefs are chosen for the administration of a band and how they were traditionally chosen. Discuss the differences and what this might mean to Native peoples.

Ask students to find out what reserves are, why Native people live on them and which Native people have the right to live on them. Ask them to consider the fact that the land is federally governed even though it is within the boundaries of a province. Ask them what implications this might have for people living on the reserves.

Contact a local band council and try to arrange a class visit to their reserve. Have students prepare questions for the band leaders.

Ask students to find out how a chief and councilors are elected on an Indian reserve. Have a classroom election of a chief and councilors.

Attitudes

Patricia Logie describes Glen Newman as an outstanding humanist. Discuss the characteristics of an outstanding humanist (Oxford Dictionary, 1984: "A person who is concerned with the study of mankind and human affairs, or who seeks to promote human welfare.") Ask students to think of someone they know who could also be described as a humanist and to prepare a speech about him or her.

Glen Newman wears "many hats". Discuss the fact that one person can have many roles and responsibilities. Ask students to consider what this might mean for their own goals and aspirations.

Aesthetic Expression

In the painting of Glen Newman, Patricia Richardson Logie has used brush work around the subject's head and shoulders to make a statement about his character. Ask students to consider what the artist is saying. Have them write poems about the painting.

Painting #12 *Chronicles of Pride* Series
Size: 26 x 34 (66.04 cm x 86.36 cm)

Simon Baker

Elder, International Native Representative

Simon Baker, an elected chief of the Squamish, is a member of the Capilano band in North Vancouver, British Columbia. He was born in 1911.

Simon Baker travels around the world with Canadian Pacific Airlines as a representative of and ambassador for the North American Indian. He has been to Japan, Germany, and the Netherlands in this capacity. When he travels he wears the costume of the Plains Indian in respect for the Plains people who gave him the headdress and have honored him as a Chief. The magnificent headdress is the most widely recognized dress of the North American Native. In the portrait, Simon Baker is wearing this costume.

Simon Baker has done much to enhance the living conditions of the people on his reserve and in his role as an elder, he teaches the young about their heritage.

Suggested Study Activities: (Simon Baker)

Knowledge, Understanding, and Abilities

Simon Baker has "traveled to many countries as an ambassador of Indian people". Discuss the purpose and impact of his duties, focusing on cultural acceptance.

In the portrait, Simon Baker wears the traditional dress of the Plains Indians. Have students research the traditional dress of other Native peoples. Students could make cutout dolls dressed in traditional clothing of various cultures, including ceremonial costumes.

Simon Baker is an elected chief of the Squamish. Ask students to find out how an elected chief differs from an hereditary chief. Have them compare current Indian government (i.e., chief and council) with traditional Indian government.

Contact a local band council and try to arrange a class visit to their reserve. Have students prepare questions for the band leaders.

Simon Baker travels a great deal. In his travels, he sometimes crosses over the border between Canada and the United States. In 1794, the *Jay Treaty* was signed, promising "nor shall any Indians passing or repassing with their own proper goods and effects of any nature, pay for the same impost or duty whatever". As a result of the Treaty, Native peoples believe they have the right to cross the border without paying duty on goods; the Supreme Court of Canada has ruled that the *Customs Act* takes precedence. Discuss the concept of the 49th parallel. Ask students to consider what effect this border would have on Native peoples whose lands are on both sides of the border (see *Maps* section). Conduct a debate about the issue of rights and customs in relation to the *Treaty* and the *Customs Act*.

Attitudes

Simon Baker wants all peoples of the world to understand the culture of his people. He travels to many different countries to fulfill this goal. Discuss why it is important to understand other people's cultures. Have students find out something about their own cultural backgrounds and prepare short talks based on the information.

Aesthetic Expression

Simon Baker stands seven and a half feet tall when he wears a headdress. Ask students what would be the impact of this and how this would make Simon Baker feel. Discuss why the artist would want to portray Simon Baker in this dress. Ask them why they think he wears this costume, even though it is the traditional dress of the Plains Indian.

Have students consider the painting of Simon Baker, looking at the artist's treatment of the different textures of the subject's costume. Have students draw or paint a series of items with different surfaces (e.g., glass jar, wood, tinfoil, piece of cloth, leather).

Painting #13 *Chronicles of Pride* Series
Size: 24 x 30 (60.96 cm x 76.2 cm)

Vivian Wilson

Fisherman, Entrepreneur

Vivian Wilson is Kwakiutl from Bella Bella in British Columbia. He was born in 1924.

Vivian is a commercial fisherman, operating a sixty-five foot seiner. He started as a young boy with a three hundred dollar fishing boat. Now, forty-five years later, he skippers his own seiner.

Vivian also established and runs an airline into remote areas of British Columbia. This all-Indian Airline is called "Waglisla". Vivian says people in many remote communities are totally isolated and have not been able to get necessary medical attention. The airline opens up some of these areas, allowing people access to emergency medical services.

Suggested Study Activities: (Vivian Wilson)

Knowledge, Understanding, and Abilities

Native peoples have always been very resourceful and able to survive using their skills and the fruits of the land. Show the film *Survival in the Bush* (see *Additional Resources*, p. 118) and discuss the survival methods used. Have students learn some traditional recipes and methods of cooking (see *Living Off The Land,* p. 93) which helped Native people survive.

Ask students to research the activities of a commercial fisherman. Have them write to the Native Indian Brotherhood (or another provincial organization) mostly concerned with fishing, to find out about the work and the issues of the fishermen.

Show the film *Salmon People* (see *Additional Resources*, p. 118). Fishing has always been the basis of the economy of Northwest Coast Native peoples. Have students to compare traditional and contemporary fishing in Native communities. Consider commerce, trading, technology, methods of preparation and preserving, the implications for amount of fish caught, and the appropriateness of the methods.

Attitudes

Vivian Wilson achieved an important goal — he established an airline which allowed residents of remote communities access to medical attention and other services from outside. Discuss the importance of this contribution to Vivian's community.

Aesthetic Expression

In the portrait of Vivian Wilson, Patricia Richardson Logie has painted the subject's "vision" in the background. Discuss the vision of the man in relation to his life. Ask students what it means to have a vision. Have them write about a personal vision which they would like to be able to realize.

Painting #16 *Chronicles of Pride* Series
Size: 30 x 36 (76.2 cm x 91.44 cm)

Paul Willie

Laboratory Technologist

Paul Willie is Kwakiutl. He is one of the hereditary chiefs of Kingcome Inlet, British Columbia, from the tribe called Datowadeno. He was born in 1944.

Paul Willie is a biochemistry technologist and is the head of the Biochemistry Laboratory at the Royal Columbian Hospital in New Westminster, British Columbia. He also lives his traditional culture as a chief of Kingcome Inlet. In this way, he lives comfortably within both Native and non-Native cultures. He believes that in order for the two societies to live in harmony, each has to learn to understand the differences and to accept those differences.

Paul Willie tells the history of his people from the time of the great flood — over 10,000 years ago. He believes that we are of the spirit world. We come into this life in physical form and then re-enter the spirit world when this life is over. He strongly believes in our ability to choose our own paths and says this choice can either lead us to be victims of circumstances, or to have some control over our circumstances.

Health is an important issue for Native peoples. Paul Willie believes that to solve health problems Native and non-Native cultures need to work together. Traditional Native cultures had a well-developed understanding of health and healing. These are in some cases different from modern notions of health and healing. Paul thinks medical knowledge would be enriched by drawing from Native and non-Native health practices.

Suggested Study Activities: (Paul Willie)

Knowledge, Understanding, and Abilities

Paul Willie is one of the "hereditary chiefs" of his area. Research how an hereditary chief differs from an elected chief. Compare current Indian government (i.e., chief and council) with traditional Indian government.

Paul Willie believes we are all of the spirit world. Show the film *The Great Spirit* (see *Additional Resources*, p. 116) which shows how many Native people are finding new strength in their traditional religious ways. Discuss the film and encourage students to find out more about the beliefs explained.

Some traditional medicines are listed in the section *Living Off The Land* (p. 95). Make copies of the information, distribute them to students, and discuss the remedies listed. Ask students if their parents have any traditions with respect to remedies and cures. Have students research the use of herbs and other remedies and write reports about their findings.

Have students research local plants that were used by the Native people for food and/or medicine. Collect plants and dry them. Display the plants on a bulletin board along with a description of their uses.

Attitudes

Paul Willie "lives comfortably within both cultures". Discuss this statement. Ask students to think about whether all Native people are able to live comfortably within both cultures.

Ask students to consider what it means to "get strength from one's spirituality". Ask them to define "spiritual". Have them write poems or draw images which illustrate their definitions. Ask them to consider why spirituality seems to play a universal role in the way people have come to understand themselves and the world in which they live.

Aesthetic Expression

Discuss the portrait of Paul Willie, noting the toned canvas. Toning a canvas is accomplished by rubbing paint onto the canvas and then rubbing it off evenly, leaving a colored canvas. There are many ways to achieve the same effect. Have students compare this background effect to others such as #4 Margo Kane (painted) and #23 Pauline Waterfall (stained).

Painting #17 *Chronicles of Pride* Series
Size 30 x 36 (76.2 cm x 91.44 cm)

Blanche Macdonald
Inspirational Leader

Blanche Macdonald was Métis. She was born in Faust, Alberta in 1931. Blanche died in 1985.

As the founder of the Blanche MacDonald Modeling School and Career College in Vancouver, British Columbia, Blanche did much for the many women who attended. She taught them the importance of self-worth in building a foundation for success in any career. She was a role model for many students — both Native and non-Native and is remembered by many for her work with children.

Blanche Macdonald helped establish a Native Communications network in British Columbia that carries Native radio programming to communities throughout the province. Many of these communities had previously no way to communicate with other parts of the province. When children went away to school for ten months, they had no immediate way of keeping in touch with their families. The communications network established by Blanche Macdonald has changed that.

Blanche Macdonald was part of the cultural group called Métis. The word "Métis" comes from the French word meaning "mixed". The ancestors of the Métis had Native mothers and European fathers — sometimes French trappers or Scottish fur traders. The Métis developed a culture distinct from Europeans and Natives. Today most of the Métis live in the three prairie provinces of Manitoba, Saskatchewan, and Alberta.

Suggested Study Activities: (Blanche Macdonald)

Knowledge, Understanding, and Abilities

Have students research the Métis people of Canada, their unique culture and contributions. Show the film *Daughters of the Country* (see *Additional Resources*, p. 116), a dramatization of the history of the Métis people. Discuss the fact that Métis people sometimes find themselves "caught between two worlds" and what that means.

Blanche Macdonald was a successful businesswoman. Have students interview business people or invite a guest speaker to class to discuss how to be successful in business. Have students think of a business they would like to start in their community and write a mock brochure to advertise it.

Discuss communication media used by society today. Explore communication systems by visiting radio stations, television stations, and newspaper offices. Ask students to write their own scripts for a class radio program. Tape it and play it for other students. Have them find and watch a television program about Native people (perhaps on Public Television).

Attitudes

Blanche Macdonald taught students about the importance of self-worth. Discuss the meaning of "self-worth", how it might be developed, and what role other people play in its development. Ask students to suggest how they can improve their own feelings of self-worth.

Discuss the importance of setting goals and how personal expectations can lead to personal achievements and can affect individuals or groups. Have students set a personal goal for the next month and after the month is up have them discuss their successes.

Aesthetic Expression

Ask students to consider the composition of the painting of Blanche Macdonald and what it means to them. Compare this composition to the composition of other paintings in the *Chronicles of Pride* Series.

Painting #19 *Chronicles of Pride* Series
Size 20 x 40 (50.8 cm x 101.6 cm)

Matthew Hill

Chief Councilor, Lay Reader, Fisherman

Matthew Hill is Tsimshian, from Kitkatla on Dolphin Island, British Columbia. He was born in 1946.

Matthew Hill studied to be a lay reader in the Okanagan and returned to his village where he assisted the parish priest in his work. He is also a fisherman and has incorporated his fishing business as Matt Hill & Sons. Matthew moved to Prince Rupert and was elected President of the Tsimshian Nation and President of the Native Indian Brotherhood in Prince Rupert.

The Tsimshian live on the part of the Northwest Coast which includes the mouths of the Skeena and Nass Rivers. They have for many years been fishermen and have grown kelp beds where they harvest herring roe. Herring roe and kelp are important to the diet of Northwest Coast peoples. Matthew Hill and others in his village ship herring roe and kelp to Japan.

Suggested Study Activities: (Matthew Hill)

Knowledge, Understanding, and Abilities

Have students research the activities of a commercial fisherman. Have them compile this information into a booklet with illustrations.

Take students to a commercial fishing harbor, a commercial fishing supplies store, a cannery, or a packers. Have students prepare questions for the staff. Ask them to make booklets to display their findings.

Bring samples of herring roe and kelp to class for the students to taste. Ask students to find out what the Japanese people do with the herring roe and kelp they buy from Canada.

Have students find out which Canadian imports and exports affect the Native Indian peoples (e.g., herring roe, kelp, fish). Take them on a tour of a port and have them question the tour guide about the goods being imported and exported.

Ask students to research the different fishing methods (traditional and contemporary) used by the Native people. Have them write reports and draw pictures of the different methods. Show the film *Salmon People* (see *Additional Resources*, p. 118).

Have students do a research project on eulachon and its importance in the diet of Northwest Coast peoples. Ask students to include methods of catching the fish and of preparing and using the eulachon oil (see *Traditional Recipes*, p. 96).

Attitudes

Matthew Hill is a lay reader, helping the parish priest in his work. This is in addition to his work as a fisherman. Ask students to consider the qualities and motivation that make a person want to take on additional responsibilities. Ask students to describe the kind of person who takes time to help others. Have them use their descriptions to write short poems about people helping people.

Aesthetic Expression

Have students consider the painting of Matthew Hill. Ask them to think about the size and shape of the painting in relation to others in the series. Ask students to describe what difference the size and shape of the canvas would mean for the artist's work. Take the students to an art gallery and have them write reviews of some of the art work.

Section V

Native Rights, Politics and Law
Marjorie Cantryn White
George Manuel
Gloria George
Judge Alfred Scow
Pauline Waterfall
Senator Len Marchand
James Gosnell, Joe Mathias, and Bill Wilson
Mildred Gottfriedson

Section Objectives

By studying the individuals portrayed in this section and engaging in the activities suggested, students will develop:

The Knowledge and Understanding

- that First Nations peoples are engaged in battles to advance their rights, through the courts and in political arenas.

- that claims on the land based on ancestral rights, education for First Nations children, the place of First Nations cultures in the Canadian Constitution, self-government, and rights of Native women are important contemporary issues which need to be addressed.

- that First Nations peoples maintain their distinct cultures and are part of the Canadian mosaic.

Abilities in

- communication, research, inquiry, problem solving, decision making

Attitudes of

- self-esteem
- respect for self and others

Painting #7 *Chronicles of Pride* Series
Size: 20 x 30 (50.8 cm x 76.2 cm)

Marjorie Cantryn White
Citizenship Court Judge

Marjorie Cantryn White is Nuu-chah-nulth. She is a member of the Ohiaht band from Port Alberni, British Columbia. She was born in 1936.

Marjorie has accomplished a great deal. She trained and worked as a practical nurse, was a founder of the Vancouver Indian Centre, was the first woman to be appointed to the Vancouver Police Commission, and sat as a judge in the Citizenship Court in Vancouver.

Marjorie Cantryn White is committed to integration. She believes that non-Indians need to be aware of the cultures of Native peoples and that integration will only be possible through the cooperation of peoples from all cultures. The idea of "integration" is for cultural groups to maintain many of their own beliefs and customs, but become part of the mainstream; at the same time, the mainstream eventually changes as the different beliefs become part of it. This policy is contrary to that proposed in the *Indian Act* when it was passed in 1892. The *Act* promoted "assimilation" which meant that cultural groups had to forsake their own beliefs and customs and adopt those of the mainstream.

Suggested Study Activities: (Marjorie Cantryn White)

Knowledge, Understanding, and Abilities

Marjorie Cantryn White believes in the integration of First Nations peoples and other Canadians. Discuss what "integration" means. Have students compare this concept with "assimilation". Ask them to consider why Native people like Marjorie Cantryn White want integration, not assimilation. Have them write an essay about the difference between the two concepts.

Discuss whether students think Native peoples can maintain their own culture and integrate as well. Invite a Native guest to speak to the class about the issues involved. Discuss the value of and the difficulties associated with integration.

When the Government of Canada passed the *Indian Act* in 1876, it intended to establish a policy of total assimilation. Native culture was to be gradually eliminated and Indians were to be sheltered and supervised until they were ready for full citizenship. Ask students to consider the effects of such policy on Native peoples. Remind them of the pride, spirituality, dignity of the people and the strength of their cultures. Ask them to write a poem or story to express how a person would feel about the policy.

Marjorie Cantryn White was a Citizenship Court Judge. Ask students to suggest what it means to be a citizen, and what it means to become a citizen of another country. If possible, take students to a citizenship court ceremony.

Attitudes

Marjorie Cantryn White has had several careers. Discuss possible reasons for this. Have students discuss their own plans for a career and to find out about the requirements of this career. Ask them to make pamphlets about their career choice and exchange them with each other.

The accomplishments of Marjorie Cantryn White are impressive. Have students consider the qualities needed to accomplish what Marjorie Cantryn White has achieved. Ask them to create short plays (or puppet plays) based on her major accomplishments. Have them perform the plays for other classes.

Have students write a story or poem about the accomplishments of someone they know. Have them give the story or poem to that person.

Aesthetic Expression

Patricia Richardson Logie says Marjorie Cantryn White is a "very small woman doing a very big job". Ask students to discuss the painting of Marjorie. Ask them if they think the artist was able to portray the subject in the way she describes her.

Painting #10 *Chronicles of Pride* Series
Size: 24 x 30 (60.96 cm x 76.2 cm)

George Manuel

*Statesman, Honorary Doctorate of Laws,
Order of Canada*

George Manuel was born on the Shuswap reserve in British Columbia. He lived from 1921 to 1989. He was a member of the Neskainlith band.

George Manuel was a leader of his people. Like all leaders in the Native tradition, he was a great orator and teacher.

George Manuel accomplished the great feat of pulling together Native peoples from across the country and helped to establish the Native Indian Brotherhood (now called the Assembly of First Nations). This body negotiated with the government over such issues as education. George Manuel believed that change comes through education. He argued for band controlled schools. He was appalled that school books and other materials ignored the cultures of the First Nations and inspired Native people to tell their own stories. He is held in great esteem for encouraging band controlled schools, for teaching Native languages, for developing history from the Native perspective, and for reclaiming the Nationhood of each Native Indian Nation. George Manuel was Grand Chief of the Union of British Columbia Indian Chiefs, and was awarded an Honorary Doctorate from the University of British Columbia.

In addition to his work with Native peoples in Canada, George Manuel traveled throughout the world and established The World Council of Indigenous People for which he was awarded the Order of Canada. This body of peoples share a common experience of having to forsake their own cultures in order to be assimilated into the established culture of the settlers. In their joining together, they are able to help one another personally and politically. George Manuel wrote a book about the situation of the indigenous peoples of the world called *Fourth World.* (see *Additional Resources*, p. 111)

Suggested Study Activities: (George Manuel)

Knowledge, Understanding, and Abilities

George Manuel worked with the indigenous peoples of the world. Have students define "indigenous" peoples. Have them write to the World Council of Indigenous People for information about the Council and its functions. Ask students to mark the locations of the different indigenous peoples on a world map. Have students research the important issues of the indigenous people of a country other than Canada and make posters to illustrate the issues (see *Additional Resources*, p. 108-113).

Show part three of the film series *Daughters of the Country* (see *Additional Resources*, p. 116) which expresses the value of education as seen through the eyes of a young girl. Discuss the film from the point of view of the young girl and the students in the class.

Native people believe strongly in having control over the education of their children. It is through education that the young will learn about their own culture and heritage, and will be able to build their own beliefs. Discuss the importance of education for passing on tradition and the consequences of being denied that right. Get a copy of the Native position paper on education (see *Additional Resources*, Native Indian Brotherhood, p. 112) and discuss the issues.

Show the film *Cold Journey* (see *Additional Resource*s, p. 115) which tells the story of a young Native boy who faces the cruelty of a white man's school and searches for meaning in his life. Discuss the importance of education which respects the value of Native culture.

Have students research the Native Indian Brotherhood (now called the Assembly of First Nations). Invite a speaker to the class to explain the role of the organization.

Attitudes

Patricia Logie discusses the traits of George Manuel and says she "painted him showing his characteristics". Discuss these traits. Ask students to explain such concepts as commitment, dedication, personal development and human dignity.

Aesthetic Expression

Have students study the painting of George Manuel, noting the expression on the subject's face and the position of his body. Ask them what they think the artist is saying about the man portrayed. Have them write a story about the kind of man he might have been.

Painting #11 *Chronicles of Pride* Series
Size: 24 x 24 (60.96 cm x 60.96 cm)

Gloria George

Lawyer

Gloria George is Wet'suwet'en. She was born at Telkwa, British Columbia.

Gloria has completed a Law Degree at the University of British Columbia. She is an activist in many Native programs and is a well-known representative of aboriginal people of Canada. She has lectured, researched for and presided over many different organizations. She has served on the Human Rights Commission and the organizing body of the World Council of Churches.

Gloria George has been involved in many political issues. She was a guest on the Canadian television show "Front Page Challenge", in connection with the *James Bay Agreement*. The *Agreement* was a land claim — the first major one since the nineteenth century. The agreement was entered into in 1975 as a consequence of the Quebec government wanting to build a series of dams. It stated that 13,700 square kilometres were owned by peoples of the Cree and Inuit Nations. A larger area of land was agreed upon for hunting rights. The agreement also stated that $225 million was to be paid to the Cree and Inuit over a twenty-five year period. Another term agreed upon was a measure of self-government for the Cree and Inuit people in the area.

Suggested Study Activities: (Gloria George)

Knowledge, Understanding, and Abilities

Show the film *Our Land is Our Life* (see *Additional Resources*, p. 117) which outlines the effects of the James Bay Power Project on the Cree prior to the *Agreement*. Discuss the issue of aboriginal rights to the land.

Ask students to research the status of the *James Bay Agreement*. Have them find out about the effects of the *Agreement* on the people involved. Ask them to determine if both parties to the *Agreement* have followed through on all the terms.

Show the film *I Was Born Here* (see *Additional Resources*, p. 116) which outlines the position of the Dene. Discuss land claims issues in your area. Collect newspaper clippings which explain the positions. Simulate a presentation to the government making the positions clear.

Show the film *The Berger Inquiry* (see *Additional Resources*, p. 115) which presents the Native peoples' position on land claims. Discuss the beliefs which are fundamental to the claims. Have students consider the viewpoints of:
- people who settled in the north
- older Native people
- younger Native people
- people who do not live in the north

Ask students to do additional research and to write to their Members of Parliament and express their own opinions on these matters.

Some current issues which affect Native peoples and others are: land claims, environmental control, status, education. Have students choose an issue to research. Ask them to write an essay or give an oral presentation on the issue.

Attitudes

Because of her achievements, Gloria George participated on a segment of "Front Page Challenge" that discussed the *James Bay and Northern Quebec Agreement* of 1975. Have students watch a segment of the television program "Front Page Challenge" in order to understand the program format. Have them simulate the program, role playing individuals in the series *Chronicles of Pride*. Ask them to consider the major accomplishments for each of the persons they portray.

Aesthetic Expression

Discuss the painting of Gloria George. Ask students to consider why Patricia Richardson Logie painted Gloria George the way she did (direction and position of light, the type of brush stroke, etc.). Ask them how the painting makes them feel about Gloria George. (The artist describes her as intelligent, quick, warm, intense.)

Painting # 20 *Chronicles of Pride* Series
Size: 28 x 34 (71.12 cm x 86.36 cm)

Judge Alfred Scow

British Columbia Provincial Court Judge

Alfred Scow was born in Alert Bay, British Columbia in 1927 and is a Kwicksutaineuk, southern Kwakiutl. He is a Kwakiutl member of the Gilford Island Band. In 1962, Alfred Scow was the first Native person to be called to the bar in British Columbia.

Alfred Scow recalls when he was a child in residential school how he was beaten for using his Native language and how he and others learned to be ashamed of their ancestry. He is happy that, like many others, he was able to rise above the trauma of those times to accomplish his goals.

Judge Scow was one of five appointed in 1967 to a land commission to study the indigenous peoples of Guyana — the Amerindians. The Commission was comprised of representatives from Canada (Judge Scow), Britain and Guyana. The members were appointed for a two year period and asked to determine who the Amerindians were, where they lived, what land they required, and to recommend the nature of the title they should have to those lands. The study was predicated upon the stated intention of the Government of Guyana to give legal title of lands to the Amerindian.

Suggested Study Activities: (Judge Alfred Scow)

Knowledge, Understanding, and Abilities

Alfred Scow was called to the Bar in 1962. Ask students to find out what this means. Discuss why there were no Indian lawyers in Canada in the early part of the 20th century.

Suggest that students write to their local university asking for information about Law programs. Invite a law student to the class and have students prepare questions for the guest.

Have students write to the University of British Columbia to find out about the First Nations House of Learning (6365 Biological Sciences Rd., University of British Columbia, Vancouver, B.C., V6T 1W5). Ask them to use the information to write reports or to make oral reports for other students in the school.

Have students research similarities and differences between Native Canadians and the Amerindians of Guyana. Have them write to the World Council of Indigenous Peoples to obtain information. Ask them to write reports or make oral reports about their findings.

Have students define "indigenous" peoples and mark the locations of the different indigenous peoples on a world map. Have them research the issues of several different indigenous groups and to compare and contrast them.

Show the film *Potlach: A Strict Law Bids Us Dance* (see *Additional Resources*, p. 117), which shows a reenactment of the "last potlatch" (see section on Agnes Alfred p. 85). Discuss the title of the film and the different kinds of laws that are depicted in the film (i.e., laws as part of a cultural tradition, laws as statutes passed by a government).

Attitudes

Ask students to find out how conflicts were resolved in Native cultures or in other cultures where there were laws written down for lawyers to interpret. Ask them to consider how they resolve conflict in their own groups of friends on the playground or on teams, etc.

Aesthetic Expression

Discuss why Patricia Richardson Logie painted Judge Scow the way she did. Ask students to consider the effect of color and what statement it makes.

Painting #23 *Chronicles of Pride* Series
Size: 24 x 30 (60.96 cm x 76.2 cm)

Pauline Waterfall
Teacher

Pauline Waterfall is Kwakiutl, of the Heiltsuk language group, from the Bella Bella Reserve, British Columbia. Born in 1944, she is descended from many chieftains.

Pauline teaches various courses for adults at the secondary school in Bella Bella. She is also an avid potter. Pauline Waterfall is interested in the history of her people and has traced her family tree, finding 396 direct descendants of her own grandmother.

Pauline Waterfall married outside her culture and lives with her husband on the outskirts of her village. In spite of her heritage as a descendant from a long line of chieftains, her decision to marry a non-Indian meant, under the *Indian Act*, that she lost her status as an Indian. That *Act*, until the passing of Bill C-31 in 1985, stated that women who married non-Indians or non-status Indians had their status revoked and were no longer entitled to live on reserve or claim other benefits under the *Act*.

Suggested Study Activities: (Pauline Waterfall)

Knowledge, Understanding, and Abilities

Have students research the *Indian Act* and the presenting and passage of Bill C-31 to find out on what basis this change was made.

Show the film *Somewhere Between* (see *Additional Resources*, p. 118) which outlines the controversy surrounding laws which discriminate against Native women. Have them discuss the feelings expressed by the women in the film.

Pauline Waterfall traced the family history of her grandmother and found 396 direct descendants, making her the matriarch of half the village. Discuss the term "matriarch". Ask students to find out what the role of the matriarch is in the culture of the Kwakiutl and what a "matrilineal" society is (lineage passed on through mother).

Attitudes

Native cultures value the extended family. Discuss the importance of the extended family to Native people. Ask students to consider their own family and the role of the various relatives. Compare any differences.

Have students research and write a report on the traditional roles of Native people in the family and in the tribe (roles of mother, grandfather, etc.).

Aesthetic Expression

Have students study the painting, noting the subject's hands. Ask students to consider why the artist would have painted them in action. Ask students to consider what the expression on Pauline's face shows.

Painting # 25 *Chronicles of Pride* Series
Size: 28 x 36 (71.12 cm x 91.44 cm)

Senator Len Marchand

Member of the Canadian Senate

Len Marchand is from the Okanagan Nation, born in 1933 on the Okanagan Reserve in Vernon, British Columbia.

Len Marchand has been involved in politics at the federal level for over twenty years. In 1968, he was elected a Member of Parliament for Kamloops/Cariboo, the second Native MP (the first was Louis Riel). He was a Member of Parliament for eleven years, serving in various ministries. In 1976, he became the first Native Cabinet Minister in his post as Minister of Small Business. Today, he is a member of the Senate.

Len Marchand was quoted in the February 20, 1989 issue of *Kahtou* on the matter of using "Indian" as a name to refer to the indigenous peoples of Canada.

> I noted with great interest in the December issue of *Kahtou* that you have come to loathe the use of the word Indian. I agree with you, and urge you to get a good national movement going to finally correct a five hundred year old error.

> The real Indians are those good citizens from India. I wonder what would have happened if Columbus was looking for China instead of India in 1492. Would we now be called Chinese?....

Senator Marchand speaks of an important issue for the First Nations peoples of this country. While each Nation has its own name which can be used to identify that particular group, it has been difficult to find an appropriate generic name to be used when speaking collectively of all First Nations people.

Suggested Study Activities: (Senator Len Marchand)

Knowledge, Understanding, and Abilities

Senator Marchand raises an important issue about the name of First Nations peoples. Discuss this issue. Discuss the meaning of aboriginal, indigenous, native. Ask students to find out what the indigenous peoples of other countries are called. Ask them to consider why Native peoples might think it inappropriate to be called Indians (Columbus' misnomer). Discuss the various labels that have been used and their own preference (see Note, p. 1 explaining the various terms used to refer to Canada's First peoples).

Many of the subjects of the portraits in *Chronicles of Pride* are educators or are primarily interested in the role of education. Len Marchand has worked as a politician. Educators and politicians believe they can change the world in different ways; educators by reaching the young, politicians by changing the laws. Discuss the different viewpoints of educators and politicians and the role each can play in advancing the rights of First Nations peoples. Have students write and present a speech from the point of view of:
  • an educator
  • a politician

Have students research the process of becoming a senator and what that job entails. Discuss the current push for an elected Senate and what this means in terms of the present government structure.

Len Marchand was the second Native Member of Parliament and Louis Riel the first. Have students research the life of Louis Riel. Ask them to defend their opinions about the justice or injustice of Riel's treatment by the government. Ask them to consider how he would be treated by today's society.

Attitudes

Contact local Native politicians and invite some of them to class. Have students prepare questions for discussion about some political issues (e.g., aboriginal rights, land claims, environmental issues, women's rights).

Organize the class for a debate on a controversial Native issue (e.g., land claims). Have a student act as chairperson or mediator.

Aesthetic Expression

Ask students to consider the painting of Senator Len Marchand by noting the color, composition, and brush strokes. Ask them what statement the artist made about the subject.

Painting #26 *Chronicles of Pride* Series
Size: 22 x 36 (55.8 cm x 91.44 cm)

James Gosnell, Joe Mathias, and Bill Wilson
A Tribute to a Unique Moment in History

The portrait shows three great Native leaders from British Columbia. The late James Gosnell was Nisga'a from Aiyansh. Joe Mathias, the Vice-Chief of the Assembly of First Nations, is Squamish from the Lower Mainland. Bill Wilson is Kwakiutl of Comox from Cape Mudge. He is coordinator of the Musgamagw Tribal Council. In 1990, Bill Wilson became Chairman of the First Nations Congress.

Together, these three men represent the body of men who traveled to Ottawa to speak to the House of Commons about the aboriginal rights clause of the Canadian Constitution. This was the first time Native people had been invited onto the floor of the House of Commons, and as such, represents an important event in Canada's history.

Aboriginal rights are based on occupation of the land prior to initial contact with Europeans. The rights claimed by the First Nations peoples of Canada are varied and include such things as claims to land, the right to self-government including education and local law enforcement, the right to protect and promote language and culture, and compensation for resources taken without the consent of the Native people involved.

First Nations peoples have had much difficulty negotiating aboriginal rights with the different levels of government. To date the *Charter of Rights and Freedoms*, Section 25 states:

> The guarantee in this Charter of certain rights and freedoms shall not be construed so as to abrogate or derogate from any aboriginal, treaty or other rights or freedoms that pertain to the aboriginal peoples of Canada...

There is agreement that treaty rights include those that might subsequently be acquired in land claims settlements. An Office of Native Claims has been established by the federal government. Land claim issues are often pursued in court. An issue still unresolved is self-government.

Knowledge, Understanding, and Abilities

The *Indian Act* is said by some to deny Indian Bands the right of self-government because it allows the Government of Canada extreme authority. Ask students to research the *Indian Act* and to be prepared to state their opinion on how it should (or should not) be changed.

In a speech to a symposium on Aboriginal Title held in Victoria in 1983, Bill Wilson said, "The only concept of title that really means anything to me ... and to other Native Indian people across the country is the feeling inside ourselves about our relationship with the land...." Ask students to explain what they think he means by that statement. Read the quote from Chief Seattle (p. 82) and ask students to relate the two ideas.

James Gosnell said, regarding the Constitutional questions, "I want my grandchildren to be able to read in history that when they patriated the Constitution and our rights were being discussed, that we were there representing our people to make the fight on behalf of title." Other Native peoples thought they should boycott the event. Discuss this issue. Ask students which position they think was right and why.

Show the film *Dancing Around the Table* (see *Additional Resources*, p. 116) which depicts the Native involvement in the Constitutional debate. Ask students to take a role from the film and to reenact the scenario from their own understanding of the issues. Ask students to find out about the debates that followed over the "Meech Lake Accord". Ask them to consider the role Elijah Harper played in defeating the Accord. Discuss the issues in the debate about the Constitution.

Collect newspaper articles which discuss issues of Native rights. Have students discuss the issues and conduct debates about the positions taken.

Attitudes

Contact local Native politicians and invite some of them to class. Have students prepare questions for discussion about some political issues (e.g., aboriginal rights, land claims).

Organize the class for a debate on a controversial Native issue (e.g., land claims). Have a student act as chairperson or mediator.

Show the film *I was Born Here* (see *Additional Resources*, p. 116). Ask the students to write and illustrate poems or stories that express the intense feelings about the land which are related in the film.

Aesthetic Expression

Discuss the composition and background of the painting and the statement made by the artist.

Painting #28 *Chronicles of Pride* Series
Size: 20 x 24 (50.8 cm x 60.96 cm)

Mildred Gottfriedson

Canadian Mother of the Year, 1964

Mildred Gottfriedson was a Shuswap from the Kamloops Reserve in Kamloops, British Columbia. She was born in 1918.

As a young woman jockey, Mildred met and married her husband who worked on a ranch in the Kamloops area. She raised twenty-three children and was grandmother to forty-five. In 1964, Mildred was named Canadian Mother of the Year.

In addition to her accomplishments with her family, Mildred Gottfriedson was involved in various political issues, especially those that affected women's rights. With the help of others, she was successful in ensuring Native women's rights at the band level. The changes to the *Indian Act* gave women the right to vote on band matters, to speak at band meetings, and to be elected as chiefs.

Mildred also addressed Section 12(1) of the *Indian Act* which stated that a woman who married a non-Indian or a non-status Indian, as well as any children she might bear, would lose their status. She did a great deal of research on the matter and could find no reason for the inclusion of this section in the *Act*.

In addition to her accomplishments with women's rights, Mildred was also instrumental in 1960 in obtaining Federal voting rights for all Native peoples.

Suggested Study Activities: (Mildred Gottfriedson)

Knowledge, Understanding, and Abilities

Section 12(1) of the *Indian Act*, until it was amended in 1985, meant that women who married non-Indians would lose their status as Indians. On the other hand, women who were non-Indian but married Indian men were granted status. Discuss the policy and consider its purpose. Have students explore the early history of government decisions involving Native women's rights.

Native cultures value the extended family. Discuss the importance of the extended family to Native people. Ask students to consider their own family and the role of the various relatives. Compare any differences.

Have students research and write a report on the traditional roles of Native people in the family and in the tribe (roles of mother, grandfather, etc.).

Show the film *Somewhere Between* (see *Additional Resources*, p. 118) which outlines the controversy surrounding laws which discriminate against Native women. Have students discuss the feelings expressed by the women in the film.

Until 1960, Native peoples had no right to vote at any level of Canadian government. Have students research this aspect of the *Indian Act* and how the *Act* was changed in this regard.

Show the film *Augusta* (see *Additional Resources*, p. 115) which shows a Shuswap grandmother telling stories of her life, or the film *Our Totem is the Raven* (see *Additional Resources*, p. 117) in which Chief Dan George explains the ways of his forefathers to a young boy. Discuss the role of elders.

Attitudes

Mildred Gottfriedson accomplished much in her life. Ask students to consider the qualities a person needs to succeed. Discuss the importance of setting goals and how personal expectations can lead to personal achievements and can affect individuals or groups. Have students set personal goals for a month and after the month is up have them discuss their successes.

Aesthetic Expression

Discuss the painting of Mildred Gottfriedson. Ask students to consider why the artist selected the pose, colors, background, etc.

Section VI

Keeping Traditions Alive
Louis Miranda
Guujaaw
David Gladstone
Agnes Alfred
Vernon Mulvahill, Don Bain, Lori Speck, Eileen Joe and Sadie Morris

Section Objectives

By studying the individuals portrayed in this section and engaging in the activities suggested, students will develop:

The Knowledge and Understanding

- that the traditional ways and distinct cultures of First Nations peoples have survived in spite of attempts by government and others to assimilate Native peoples into the mainstream culture.

- that there is a conscious effort on the part of First Nations peoples to maintain and preserve their ways and beliefs.

- that pride in their heritage is an important feature of First Nations cultures.

Abilities in

- communication

- research

- inquiry, problem solving, decision making

Attitudes of

- self-esteem

- respect for self and others

Painting #6 *Chronicles of Pride* Series
Size: 20 x 24 (50.8 cm x 60.96 cm)

Louis Miranda

Honorary Doctorate of Laws

Louis Miranda, a Squamish, was born in North Vancouver, British Columbia in 1892, and until he was ninety-eight years of age, was still teaching there. He was one of the last of his Nation who lived in the traditional ways of his people.

Louis Miranda worked with linguists to develop an orthography for his language. A system of writing allows a culture's language to be preserved where it might otherwise become extinct. Many Native languages are on the verge of becoming extinct because so few people speak them. Louis Miranda's accomplishment will mean that the Squamish language can be preserved in written form.

As a respected elder of the Squamish Nation, Louis Miranda taught Squamish language, history and culture to students in North Vancouver. For his work, Simon Fraser University granted him an Honorary Doctorate of Laws.

The painting of "Uncle" Louis, as he is called fondly by his associates, was completed in one sitting. This is an unusual circumstance, but as Patricia Richardson Logie explains, she "attacked" the painting and worked as quickly as possible because Louis would not move or take a rest. The cooperation, commitment, and perseverance reflected in Louis Miranda's actions are traditional values of the culture.

Suggested Study Activities: (Louis Miranda)

Knowledge, Understanding, and Abilities

Louis Miranda was awarded an Honorary Doctorate from Simon Fraser University. Have students write to the University to find out how and why such degrees are bestowed.

Have students listen to some recordings or look at written examples of Native languages (see *Additional Resource*s, p. 118). Have students make an illustrated dictionary of some Native words. Invite a guest to speak to the students and to teach them some words in a Native language. Have students prepare questions for the guest about his or her own language. Ask students to consider how their own languages are passed down from generation to generation. Ask them what would happen if we did not have writing.

Ask students to make a list of place names in their area which came from Native languages.

Discuss the fact that at one time missionary schools and residential schools forbade Native children to speak their own language. (If possible, watch the CBC production called "Where the Spirit Lives".) Ask students to imagine how this restriction made the children feel. Ask students who have English as a second language to share any similar experiences they may have had. Have students write about different ways people manage to preserve their own language (e.g., schools, homes, media).

Explain to students that language is constantly changing. Ask them to make a list of words which are popular with their peers today. Have them interview older siblings or other relatives to discover what words were popular when they were young. Ask students to compare the two lists and to speculate about the reasons for the differences.

Have students consider the different sounds used in Native languages, in English, and in any other language with which the students are familiar. Have them note the differences.

Attitudes

"Uncle" Louis Miranda portrayed characteristics that are very important to his people: perseverance, cooperation, commitment, and respect. Discuss why it is important to possess these traits. Read some legends that illustrate these traits. Ask students to write legends or draw pictures which illustrate the importance of these characteristics. Have students consider why people would call Louis Miranda "Uncle", even if they were not relatives.

Aesthetic Expression

Discuss the portrait of Louis Miranda, noting the toned canvas. Toning is accomplished by rubbing paint onto the canvas and then rubbing it off evenly, leaving a colored surfaced. There are many ways to achieve this affect. Have students compare this background effect to others such as #4 Margo Kane (painted) and #23 Pauline Waterfall (stained).

Painting #21 *Chronicles of Pride* Series
Size: 24 x 36 (60.96 cm x 91.44 cm)

Guujaaw

Hunter and Gatherer of Food

Gary Edenshaw wants to be known by his Haida name of Guujaaw, a potlatch name meaning drum. He is Haida, from Masset on Haada Gwaaii (the Queen Charlotte Islands). He was born in 1953.

Guujaaw refuses to accept the name given to him in the European tradition. Names are important in the Haida culture. They are given in formal ceremonies and indicate position, identity and responsibilities, and provide guidance. Missionaries and government officials did not understand the significance and imposed names which meant nothing to the Native people. For many years, Natives were not permitted to register their own names.

Guujaaw, as Patricia Logie says, embodies the romance of the Native Indian people. He is a carver, a carpenter, a dancer, and a singer. When in his homeland on the Queen Charlottes he lives by the land and the sea, much as his ancestors did.

Guujaaw has fought along with his people to save their land. In Native culture, there is a different concept of land from that of Europeans. While Europeans think of owning the land and taming it for their use, the Native people see the earth as mother and all creatures as her children. There is a responsibility to care for the land, to share its riches with all things, living and nonliving, and to ensure that the same riches will be accessible to their children.

Suggested Study Activities: (Guujaaw)

Knowledge, Understanding, and Abilities

Discuss why Gary Edenshaw prefers to be known by his Haida name, Guujaaw. Have students research the importance of naming in Native cultures.

Contact local Native politicians and invite them to class. Have students prepare questions for discussion about some political issues (e.g., aboriginal rights, land claims, environmental issues, women's rights).

Chief Seattle, in 1852, said

> ...This we know. The earth does not belong to man: man belongs to the earth. This we know. All things are connected like the blood which unites one family. All things are connected. Whatever befalls the earth befalls the sons of the earth. Man did not weave the web of life, he is merely a strand in it. Whatever he does to the web, he does to himself...

This statement reflects the beliefs of many First Nations people. Discuss what it means. Ask students to suggest why environmental concerns would arise from these beliefs. Ask them to choose an environmental issue to research and relate the issue to the interconnectedness of all things. Show the film *I Was Born Here* (see *Additional Resources*, p. 116), a tribute to the intense relationship between the people and the land.

Guujaaw is a hunter and a gatherer of food, as were his ancestors — taking care of the land because he is dependent on it. Have students find out about traditional methods of fishing and hunting of the Haida people by researching the following questions:

• What were the main staples of the Haida people?

• How were the various parts of a salmon put to use?

• What plants did the people use/eat?

• How did the seasons affect the food habits of the Haida?

• How were foods preserved?

Have students research the hunting and food gathering of other Nations in Canada and compare their findings. Have them do a seasonal timeline where they enter the various activities for each season.

Attitudes

Guujaaw lives by the beliefs of his ancestors. He wishes to preserve a life that respects and understands the complex relationships in the ecosystem. Ask students to write environmental groups to find out what beliefs they hold, and have students compare these with Guujaaw's.

Aesthetic Expression

Ask students to study the painting of Guujaaw. Have them describe how the painting relates to what they know about the man.

Painting #22 *Chronicles of Pride* Series
Size: 28 x 36 (71.12 cm x 91.44 cm)

David Gladstone
Native Historian

David Gladstone is Heiltsuk from Bella Bella, British Columbia. He was born in 1955.

David is a young man who has learned the ways of his people from the elders. In turn, he teaches language to the young people of his village and plays a role of linking the old with the new. He is immersed in the traditions of his culture and has plans to establish a museum in the local secondary school to house a collection of artifacts and costumes.

David Gladstone represents the growing interest of young Native people in their traditions. At one time, villages were determined to adopt the ways of the white people and denied their own heritage. This route led to much unhappiness. By learning the language and other aspects of their culture, David and others are preserving the valuable heritage of their people, promoting respect for this heritage and enhancing the lives of Native peoples and others.

In the portrait, David wears a traditional costume of the Heiltsuk. His mother made the Chilkat blanket and his aunt the apron with pounded pennies and quarters.

Suggested Study Activities: (David Gladstone)

Knowledge, Understanding, and Abilities

Wearing traditional costumes and dancing the ritual dances are rights which must be earned in the Heiltsuk culture. Have students find out what one must do to "earn the right" to wear the traditional costumes and perform the songs and dances.

The potlatch is central to Northwest Coast Native culture. In other cultures, pow wow, longhouse feasts or other similar ceremonies constitute the same kind of event. The potlatch is governed by strict laws which are taught to all by the elders. It is held to commemorate an important event such as a marriage, a death, the raising of a totem pole, the giving of a name, or the building of a new house. A potlatch involves a feast, a ceremony of songs, stories and dances, and it culminates in the giving of gifts. Have students research the potlatch. Have them find out why the Canadian government banned the events.

Show the video *Box of Treasures* (see *Additional Resources*, p. 115) and discuss First Nations peoples' reaction to their sacred objects being taken by the government. Have students consider why David Gladstone would be interested in establishing a museum in his community. Have them write to museums in their area to ask about the Native artifacts in their collections: where they come from, how they were acquired, etc.

Attitudes

David Gladstone is a young man who has made it his goal to uncover and preserve the traditions of his people. Ask students what they think are his reasons for doing this. Show the film *The Great Spirit* (see *Additional Resources*, p. 116) which shows that many Native peoples are gaining strength from their traditional ways. Discuss this idea.

Aesthetic Expression

Using the Vancouver School Board publication and tape *People of the Salmon* (see *Additional Resources*, p. 119), teach children some Native songs and their significance.

Songs and dances are important parts of all Native ceremonies and each has special significance. Play some Native songs for students. Have them draw pictures to illustrate the images the songs evoke. Watch some Native dance, if possible, and discuss its importance in the ceremonies of the people.

Have students consider the painting of David Gladstone. Ask them to what the background in this painting might relate(i.e., the passage from the old to the new). Have students compare David's dress to that of Simon Baker and Leonard George.

Painting #30 *Chronicles of Pride* Series
Size: 24 x 30 (60.96 cm x 76.2 cm)

Agnes Alfred
Elder

Agnes Alfred was born on Village Island near Alert Bay, British Columbia. At ninety-odd years, she is one of the few remaining traditional elders of a Native culture. She does not know her actual birth date, but it is recorded on a rock on Village Island.

An elder is highly respected by Native peoples. It is the elder who passes on the history of the people through songs, stories, customs and rules.

Agnes Alfred was part of a potlatch in 1922, often mistakenly referred to as the "last potlatch". In 1884, the federal government had declared potlatches illegal and prohibited them under heavy penalties. The ban was not lifted until 1951. Agnes was jailed for her participation in the 1922 ritual which stands out as an important event because of the harsh penalties applied.

The potlatch is central to Northwest Coast Native culture. It is governed by strict laws which are taught by the elders. The potlatch is held to commemorate an important event such as a marriage, a death, the raising of a totem pole, the giving of a name, or the building of a new house. A potlatch involves a feast, a ceremony of songs, stories and dances, and culminates in the giving of gifts. The host gives gifts to those who come, thus distributing his wealth and increasing his status. Generosity is a sign of greatness. Guests, in their turn, hold a potlatch and share their wealth.

Suggested Study Activities: (Agnes Alfred)

Knowledge, Understanding, and Abilities

Contact a local band council and try to arrange a class visit to their reserve. Ask to meet some of their elders. Have students prepare questions for the elders. Tape record and photograph the elders if allowed.

Show the film *Augusta* (see *Additional Resources*, p. 115), in which a Shuswap grandmother tells stories from her life, or the film *Our Totem is the Raven* (see *Additional Resources*, p. 117), in which Chief Dan George explains the ways of his forefathers to a young boy. Discuss the place of elders.

Show the film *Potlatch: A Strict Law Bids Us Dance* (see *Additional Resources*, p. 117) which recreates the "last potlatch" in 1922. Discuss the importance of potlatch to Northwest Coast Native cultures. In other cultures, pow wow, longhouse feasts, or other similar ceremonies constituted the same kind of event. Ask students to imagine they were living in 1884 when the government ban was declared. People mistakenly refer to the Potlatch of 1922 as the "last potlatch". In fact, many Native people continued their tradition in secret. Have students write to the government to express their opinions about the tradition of the potlatch.

Using British Columbia Teachers' Federation Lesson Aid #2011 *To Potlatch or Not to Potlatch* (see *Additional Resources*, p. 113), distribute articles to groups of students. Have them take one of the positions (a government official recommending the banning of the potlatch, Chief Maquinna appealing to the government to lift the ban, etc.) and debate the issues as presented.

Attitudes

Discuss what wealth meant to traditional Native people. Ask students to compare this view with what wealth means to the average North American today.

Aesthetic Expression

Storytelling is an important part of First Nations cultures because their history is passed on through their stories. Provide students with legends and myths to read. Ask them to tell the stories in their own words to others in the class. Have students dramatize stories, and create dances or music to accompany them.

Show the film *The Man, the Snake and the Fox* (see *Additional Resources*, p. 117) which uses masks to dramatizes a legend. Have students create masks to accompany Native legends.

Have the class make a totem pole — you could use papier mache or other materials. Erect the totem pole and have a celebratory potlatch for the class or the school. Make or donate gifts to give away at the potlatch.

Ask students how they feel about the painting of Agnes Alfred. Ask them to consider in their appraisal: color, composition, brush strokes, statement, etc.

Painting #31 *Chronicles of Pride* Series
Size: 48 x 48 (121.92 cm x 121.92 cm)

Vernon Mulvahill, Don Bain, Lori Speck Eileen Joe, and Sadie Morris
A Promise

The final portrait of the series is of Vernon Mulvahill, Don Bain, Lori Speck, Eileen Joe, and Sadie Morris, five young members of the Native Youth Program of the University of British Columbia Museum of Anthropology.

The Native Youth Program is run by the University of British Columbia Museum of Anthropology. It is open to all Native young people, between the ages of fourteen and seventeen. Candidates who are selected as part of the program learn about the traditions of their people. They also act as guides in the Museum of Anthropology and speak to groups about their cultures.

Patricia Richardson Logie calls this painting "A Promise", because in the young she sees promise for the future of the Native cultures of Canada. The young people reflect the dynamic nature of the cultures — knowledge and respect for traditional customs, combined with a modern lifestyle.

Suggested Study Activities: (A Promise)

Knowledge, Understanding, and Abilities

Education does not only take place in institutions such as schools. In Native cultures, the elders are the teachers of the traditional ways. Show the films *Kevin Alex* and *Our Totem is the Raven* (see *Additional Resources*, p. 116, 117) which depicts young Natives learning about their traditional ways. Ask students to write or tell stories about important things they have learned in places other than school.

Ask students to research the traditional roles of Native people in the family and the tribe (roles of mother, son, grandfather, etc.). Have them compare those roles to contemporary roles of family members.

Have students write to a school for Native students (contact a local Native organization for school locations) to ask for a pen-pal with whom they can exchange information about their culture and their education.

Ask students to compare the lifestyle of their parents when they were young to their own life-styles. Ask them to do "then-and-now" pictures.

Have students find out if there is a program for Native youth in your area. (For example, a Native Youth Program is sponsored by the University of British Columbia Museum of Anthropology). If so, invite a member of the group to visit the class to speak about the program. Ask students to make oral reports about their findings.

Attitudes

Ask students to think about their own futures. Ask them to suggest what they could do today to give their own futures promise. Have them draw or write about their own visions for the future and encourage them to keep these for later reading or viewing.

Aesthetic Expression

Discuss the painting "A Promise". Ask students to suggest why the artist chose that title. Focus a discussion on what students think are the attributes that promote a feeling of promise; on what they see in the eyes of the subjects; what they believe these young people could be when they mature; what they believe Native children could accomplish that would help their people. Discuss why Native children are considered the first natural resource.

Section VII

Additional Study Activities

The following activities can be incorporated into the study of any of the subjects. They are included here because of their general nature. They may be selected for use in a culminating activity.

Knowledge, Understandings, and Abilities

- Develop a vocabulary list derived from the collection.

- Write a conversation that could have taken place between the artist and one of the models during the painting.

- Subscribe to a Native newspaper. (see *Native Periodicals*, p. 122)

- Make a "Big Book", complete with illustrations about one of the subjects from the collection, depicting the subject's achievements.

- Write and illustrate Native legends using characters from Native legends. Display the legends on a bulletin board or make them into a book for the library.

- Create a book as a group activity on a topic pertinent to the subjects in the collection. Each group could have a writer, illustrator, researcher, photocopier, binder, etc.

- Write a speech from the viewpoint of the subjects in the portraits. The speech could be on personal achievements, leadership traits, or tribal group. Present the speech to the class or to another class. Speeches could be tape recorded or videotaped.

- Create short plays (or puppet plays) based on the major accomplishments of the individuals in the *Chronicles of Pride* series. Perform them for other classes.

- Choose two subjects from the collection (e.g., Robert Sterling and Walter Harris). Compare and contrast their cultures, languages, professions and/or political views.

- Write to a Native school asking for a pen-pal (contact a local Native organization school locations).

- Discuss similarities and differences of the cultures of two of the subjects in the series (e.g., Upper Salish and Cree). Examine: environment, language, food, traditional and contemporary lifestyles.

- Visit a museum of anthropology with a list of questions pertaining to the cultural groups of the subjects.

- Select one interesting aspect that the subjects have in common (e.g., respect for the environment, respect for all living things). Discuss.

- Discuss similarities and differences in lifestyles of the various cultures living within Canada.

- Create a skit or play involving the achievements of some of the subjects in the collection. Puppets could be made and used.

- Complete a research project: for example, respect for the environment is something that all subjects of *Chronicles of Pride* have in common. Explore ways the community helps to keep a healthy environment. Interview people working in factories, fast food restaurants, ranches, dairy farms, etc. Make booklets on "ways to keep a healthy environment". Provide each company or organization visited with a copy of the booklet.

- Research the subgroupings of some of the cultural groups such as Haisla-Kwakiutl or Gitksan Wet'suwet'en, focusing on the group's distinct identity within a geographical group.

- Invite Native guests to give mini-workshops or presentations to the class. A suggested "theme" format could be used (e.g., accomplishments of artists, political issues, educational programs).

- Have a mini career day. The class could be divided into groups for planning. Each group could invite guests to set up a booth relating to specific careers.

- Research the career of one of the people in the series, or a career of personal interest. Prepare for the class an information package about the career researched.

- Research leadership roles played by some contemporary Native women.

- Research the educational requirements of careers of interest.

- Write to colleges and universities asking for information about their programs and requirements.

- Make a pamphlet describing one profession. Share with the class.

- Complete more in depth research activities on the following career areas: art, acting, business, theology, politics, medicine, law, and education.

Attitudes

- Develop a *Chronicles of Pride* using family members. Focus on each individual's accomplishments, endeavors and dreams. Pictures and photographs could be used. Recognize all accomplishments, great and small.

- Create a biography of one of the subjects in the series, listing personal data and focusing on the individual's achievements. This could be accompanied by a drawing, painting, or clay bust of the subject.

- Research the cultural background and achievements of one of the subjects in the *Chronicles of Pride* series. Gather information from books, newspapers, people, films, videos belonging to educational institutions or government agencies, etc. Share the information with the class.

- Using a collection of articles and film clips about Native peoples and current issues, examine the media's portrayal of Native peoples, looking for biased and unbiased reporting.

Aesthetic Expression

- Make puppets of legend characters (e.g., Raven, Thunderbird, Killer Whale). Using the puppets, act out familiar legends.

- Visit a display of portraits. Research the reason the artist painted the subject (e.g., beauty, accomplishments).

- Research and use an art form to show a particular theme (e.g., fall scene in oil pastels, head sculptured in clay, winter scene in charcoal and white chalk).

- Make posters or collages depicting a chosen subject's profession or accomplishments.

- Create a photo essay by photographing accomplishments of families, neighbors, classmates or other students in the school and displaying them in a form that makes a statement.

- Make a poster depicting a chosen profession. Have a poster contest.

- Invite an artist to class to discuss and demonstrate form, line, shapes, colors, techniques and styles.

- Choose a color such as "red". Write a poem about that color, beginning with "Red makes me feel..." or "Red reminds me of..." Paint a picture and display the poetry with the painting.

- Find out about one or more of the following with regard to the *Chronicles of Pride* series:

    why the artist used various sizes of canvas

where the action is in each painting

why the artist used certain colors

what the colors mean to Native peoples

the compositions, movement, colors, and reasons for the areas painted

what statement the artist is making in the individual paintings

what statement the artist is making with the whole series

areas in which art can be used to make a statement (e.g., politics, religion, humor)

the significance of the artist's subject matter in this series.

- Create a painting to express an impression of a subject. As Patricia Richardson Logie has, use particular colors and tones to symbolize or emphasize certain traits of each subject.

- Compare and contrast two or more paintings from the series.

- Research the art work done by one or more of the subjects in the collection (e.g., Daphne Odjig, Walter Harris, Lyle Wilson, Pauline Waterfall, Guujaaw).

- Visit a local art gallery looking for art styles and forms previously discussed.

Art Appreciation:

- Research various styles, expressions and mediums in art.

- Research schools of thought in art (e.g., academic, impressionism, cubism, fauvism, expressionism).

- Research an artist from each "school", give the name of the artist, the period, the medium and what the artist is known for.

- Research English, American, Dutch, and French portrait painters (e.g., Augustus John, John Singer Sargent, Frans Hals, Eugene Delacroix).

- Research portraiture: history, composition, colors, and reasons for the artist's concept.

- Study the figure in action. Discuss body movement and body language.

- Create an "Art Collection" using paintings, photographs or drawings. Give the collection a title. Discuss the terms "series" and "collection". Put on an art show. Prepare introductions for the art collections.

Section VIII

Living Off The Land:
Activities and Information about Traditional Ways

Activities in this section can be used to study the traditional ways of the First Nations peoples.

Students could be asked to:

• Pretend they are alone in the forest without supplies because of a plane crash and find out what they could use for food and shelter.

• Collect soapberries. Find out how to make "Indian ice cream". Make some for the class (see p. 98).

• Prepare and serve a meal of traditional Native foods (e.g., moose, deer, salmon, bannock, berries).

• Make bannock (see p. 99).

• Obtain information on Native cultural foods and find out which foods are still abundantly used and which foods are no longer available.

• Compare and contrast foods of two or more cultures.

• Research the traditional foods of a Native Indian tribe from Western Canada and the foods of a tribe from Eastern Canada. Compare these foods to our contemporary diet. Create a chart of Native Indian foods based on the Canada Food Guide's four categories.

• Create a mural depicting the hunting, fishing, and food preservation methods of a Native group.

• Dramatize a deer hunt or a salmon fishing trip.

• Label a picture of a deer (or other animal) to show how every part of the animal was used by the Native people.

• Label a picture of a salmon (or other fish) to show how every part of the fish was used by the Native people.

• Research how Native people met their needs by trading.

• Find out the procedures involved in tanning hides.

- Make replicas or sketches of traditional Native tools and weapons.

- Research different types of shelter used by Native people in summer and in winter.

- Research seasonal changes in clothing, food, shelter, activities, location (e.g., how summer clothing differed from winter clothing).

The following is a description of a program in North Vancouver that gives students the opportunity to experience some of the traditional ways of the Squamish. Find out if any such programs exist in your own area.

Squamish Longhouse Program

A Squamish cultural immersion program available through School District #44 (North Vancouver) in British Columbia allows students to be a part of the Longhouse Program. Students may spend a specific length of time (usually two days) living in the Longhouse to learn how the Native Indians lived.

Objectives of the Program

- To enhance the students' understanding of and respect for Native Indian culture in general and the pre-contact longhouse culture of the Squamish people in particular.

- To provide a cultural program which will allow students:

    a) to live in a Coast Salish longhouse, built and furnished as it would have been in pre-contact times

    b) to participate in the activities and the traditional daily lifestyle of the Coast Salish people of the Squamish Valley during that time, and

    c) to learn how to use the culture's artifacts.

- To make available a variety of activities that will create a greater understanding of the beliefs and attitudes of the Coast Salish culture in relation to: sharing, the seasons, respect for others, and nature.

- To participate in activities with the Native people of the Squamish area at the longhouse site.

Medicinal Plants

Waxberry
- berries mashed and used as a poultice for children's skin, to relieve itching, to cure running eyes and as an antiperspirant

Kinnikinnick
- berries and leaves used to cure diarrhea.
- leaves and stems boiled to make a medicine for use as:
    wash for sore eyes
    tonic for kidneys and bladder
    remedy for spitting blood
    to eliminate dandruff
    to cure scalp diseases
    a wash for skin sores

Soapberry Branches
- boiled to make:
    laxative
    stomach medicine
    shampoo
    cure for poison ivy rash
    contraceptive

Raspberry
- berries eaten fresh, dried or crushed as juice
- branches boiled as tea for heartburn or diarrhea
- roots boiled as tea for constipation

Bitter-root
- used to treat:
    external eye sores
    diabetes
    poison ivy rash

Soapberries
- used to make "Indian ice cream"

Blackroot
- used as a remedy for asthma

Dandelion
- leaves eaten as a vegetable

Sage
- leaves and branches boiled to make a medicine for:
    colds
    sore throats
    tonsillitis

Sagebrush Bark
- used to:
    make quivers for arrows
    make saddle blankets
    make dresses
    make breechclouts
    start fires
    smoke hides

Saskatoon Berries
- eaten as fruit
- mixed with salmon eggs

Saskatoon Branches
- boiled to make tea
- used as a medicine for colds
- used for arrows and spears
- used to make rope

Chokecherries
- used to make jelly to mix with other foods

Traditional Recipes

Smoked salmon, barbecued salmon, pan fried eulachons, sunflower roots, briar shoots, dried berries, sun-dried berries, Indian ice cream,wild rose jelly, bannock, wild rose tea, dried seaweed, boiled dried seaweed.

Smoked Salmon

1. Remove the head of the salmon by cutting across the back from gill to gill.

2. Do not scale the fish.

3. To open the salmon cut the back along both sides of the backbone.

4. Pull the backbone away from the meat and remove the insides.

5. Open the fish flat.

6. Cut 5 mm (1/4 in.) slices from the fish in areas where the meat is thickest; i.e., midway between the outer edge and the backbone area. Do not cut through the skin. Take one or two slices about 15 cm (6 in.) long and 5 cm (2 in.) wide from each side of the salmon. This helps the meat to dry evenly and prevents spoilage in the thicker areas. Some people completely remove the thin meat slices while others keep them attached at the tail.

7. Leave a thick strip of meat, about 1 cm (½ in.) wide, all along the outer edge of the fish. Three sharpened cedar sticks, about the thickness of a pencil, are placed across the fish to hold it open. The ends of the sticks are embedded in the thick outer rim of the meat. Work quickly as the fish tends to fall apart if exposed to the air too long.

8. Hang the fish by the tail in the smokehouse. To do this push a cedar stick through the flat part of the fish at the base of the tail. Let it hang in the centre of the cedar stick which then rests on two poles of the smokehouse rack.

9. Half-smoked salmon requires one to three days smoking; fully-smoked salmon may require four or more days. Traditionally, the fish was pounded several times a day during the smoking period to make it soft. Also any small bones left in the meat were removed. When the smoking has been completed, sprinkle salt on the meat and store it for the future.

10. Before serving fully-smoked salmon, soak it overnight then steam it for twenty minutes. Fully-smoked salmon may also be toasted. Take the whole fish from the smokehouse or from winter stores, hold it by the fins and move it back and forth over the open fire until it is hot and crisp.

Pan-Fried Eulachons

Fresh eulachons can be fried for serving. Wash the fish, flour them, then fry in shortening or oil. Many people do not feel that it is necessary to clean the fish or remove the bones.

Sunflower Roots (Balsam Root)

The "sunflower" plant is commonly seen on slopes in the dry southern interior of British Columbia, in the East Kootenays and southern areas of Vancouver Island. It resembles the cultivated sunflower but is much smaller. The flowers are 7.5 cm (3 in.) across and the plant is about 30.5 cm (12 in.) high. The taproot, which is about 30.5 cm (12 in.) long, is dug in the spring and used for food. The outer skin is peeled off before the roots are cooked. Traditionally the roots were cooked in pits; now they are steamed in a pot on top of the stove. Steamed "sunflower roots" are served hot as a vegetable.

Briar Shoots

The new shoots of briar-like bushes (salmon berry, thimble berry) are peeled, dipped in sugar and eaten raw.

Dried berries

Before home canning became a widely used method of food preservation, drying was the main way to keep food through the winter. Berries were dried whole, after crushing or after they were boiled.

Sun-dried Berries

Berries such as huckleberries, blueberries, wild cranberries and saskatoon berries were placed on mats to dry in the sun for several days. Today, berries are usually dried on canvas. When the berries are hard and dry, they may be stored in a cool dry place for winter use.

To serve:

1. Soak the berries overnight in fresh water.
2. Boil for a few minutes.
3. Serve with eulachon grease and sugar.

Wild Rose Jelly

The ripe fruit or hips of wild roses make an excellent jelly. This jelly is high in Vitamin C.

1. Boil under tender: 450 g (1 lb.) rose hips, 250 ml (½ pt.) water

2. Sieve the pulp and add: 450 g (1 lb.) sugar for each 450 g (1 lb.) pulp

3. Return the rose hip mixture to boil until it jells. The jelly point is reached when the jelly breaks in a sheet or flake from a cool spoon dipped in the mixture.

Indian Ice Cream

Indian ice cream is a traditional fruit dish made from soopallalie (buffalo or soap) berries. Long ago the berries were gathered by placing a cedar bark mat under the bushes. When the bushes were hit the berries would fall onto the mat. From there, they were put in wooden boxes which were made especially for carrying berries. After gathering, the berries were rolled down a damp board. The berries would fall into a basket but the twigs, leaves and dirt would stick to the board.

Before beaters were used people would use their hands to whip up the berries. The hands and arms were scrubbed as well as the boxes used for making ice cream so that no grease would come in contact with the berries. Grease would prevent foam from forming.

Method:

1. In a clean metal, porcelain or glass bowl combine: 30 ml (2 T) canned, soopallalie berries, 120 ml (½ C) of water

2. Beat until a foam forms. Gradually add: 45-60 ml (3-4 T) of sugar (up to 120 ml (½ C) may be added if desired)

3. Continue beating until the foam is stiff. Serve immediately.

serves 4-6.

Note: If fresh berries are used, 250 ml (1 C) of fresh berries is equal to 30 ml (2 T) of canned. Crush 30 ml (2 T) fresh berries and mix with 60 ml (¼ C) of cold water. Begin beating the mixture then add the remainder of the cup of fresh berries. Follow the above recipe beginning at step 2.

Wild Rose Tea

Remove the bark from wild rose bushes. Peel off the inner bark. Cut the inner bark in tiny pieces and pour boiling water over it. Allow the tea to steep to desired strength.

Bannock

Bannock was introduced to the Native population by early explorers and missionaries. It is often used now as a substitute for yeast bread, especially in areas where commercially produced bread is not available or is very expensive.

Basic Bannock

Oven temperature 218°C (425°F)

In a large bowl combine: 1000 ml (4 C) flour, 14 ml (3 Tsp) baking powder, 2.5 ml (½ Tsp) of salt

Mix dry ingredients well and add a mixture of: 180 ml (¾ C) evaporated milk, 180 ml (¾ C) water

Gently combine the ingredients to form a soft dough, then knead eight or ten times. Overworking the dough gives a tough bannock. Place the dough on a floured surface and press into a circle about 1 cm (½ in.) thick. Make 4cm (1½ in.) long cuts halfway through the dough with a knife. Make the cuts 5 cm (2 in.) apart.

Bake the bannock on aluminum foil or a cookie sheet for 20-25 minutes. When done it will be golden brown in color. Cool the bannock under a towel for ten minutes. Cut into wedges or squares and serve warm with margarine and homemade jam.

Notes: Bannock dipped in seal grease is reported to be delicious. 30 ml (2 T) shortening or bear fat cut into the flour makes a more tender bannock.

Nutritional notes: An egg, beaten slightly, may be added with the milk to the bannock dough. Bannock may be made with whole wheat flour.

Bonfire Bannock

Prepare the basic dough. Press out the dough according to directions, but make it 6 mm (¼ in.) thick. Cut in strips one inch wide. Wind the dough, spirally, around a stick about 1 cm (½ in.) thick. Holding the stick about 20 cm (8 in.) from the fire, rotate it slowly until the bannock is golden brown.

Camp Bannock

Bannock can also be cooked in a frying pan next to the campfire. Follow the recipe for basic bannock but press the dough to 6 mm (¼ in.) thick and cut into circles. Lean the frying pan against a rock or logs so that it faces the fire at an angle. The bannock should be from 15 to 20 cm (6 to 8 in.) from the fire depending on the heat. Cook until the top is brown; turn over, and continue cooking until the second side is brown.

Fried Bannock

Prepare the basic bannock dough, rolling it slightly thinner. Cut out circles or squares about 7.5 cm (3 in.) in diameter. Deep fry in 4 cm (1½ in.) of oil until golden brown. Serve warm.

Seaweed

In May some of the people of Kincolith gather seaweed on Wales Island in Portland Inlet. The seaweed is picked from the rocks on the beaches at low tide. It is about 2.5 cm (1 in.) wide and 30.5 cm (12 in.) long and dark green in color.

Dried Seaweed

Spread the seaweed on mats or canvas in the sun to dry for two to three days. Do not dry it indoors or allow it to get wet as this causes rotting. When the seaweed is dry, leave it in chunks or cut it in pieces, cover and store in a cool dark place. Serve dried seaweed in chunks to be dipped in eulachon grease, or serve it boiled or toasted.

Historical Pit Cooking

Many of the older Native people throughout British Columbia remember watching their mothers use steaming pits to cook food. The pit varied in size and design in different areas, but the basic method was the same.

In the Southern Cariboo, the pits were made large enough to allow four to six women to cook their food together. A pit was dug 1.22 m x 3.66 m x 3.66 m (4 ft. x 6 ft. x 6 ft.).

Sticks, 7.5 cm (3 in.) thick, were laid across the top of the pit. Stones, 15 cm (6 in.) thick, were placed on top of the sticks. One man reported that stones from the bottom of the stream bed would crack and should not be used. A fire of fir, alder or cottonwood was built on top of the stones. The fire heated the stones and burned the supporting sticks, releasing the rocks which fell into the bottom of the pit. The hot embers and stones were spread with a stick evenly over the bottom of the pit.

Sticks, about 2.5 cm (1 in.) thick and 1 m (4 ft.) long, were stuck on the pit floor between red hot stones. The upper end of the sticks should be above the top of the pit.

Next, the hot rocks and embers were covered with a 5 cm (2 in.) layer of earth. Small twigs of maple bushes, service berry bushes or rose bushes were spread over this layer of earth. These twigs were added to give a sweet flavor to food as it steamed.

Washed timber grass was placed over the flavoring twigs to keep food clean. Mats of closely woven cedar bark or bullrushes were placed on top of the timber grass and around the sides of the put.

Each woman would place her food on top of the mats in a special area. The selection of food and the amounts to be cooked were important because the cooking time would be the same for all; i.e., it would not be possible for one woman to cook a 12 cm (4¼ in.) level of camas roots while her neighbor was cooking a 25 cm (9½ in.) layer. Food was shared so that each woman would have approximately the same amount to cook.

Mats and flavoring sticks were placed on top of the food. A layer of damp timber grass was laid over the flavoring sticks. Earth was piled on the grass until the pit was filled to ground level.

The sticks sticking out from the hot rocks were moved from side to side to slightly enlarge the holes. A small amount of cold water was poured down the enlarged holes to produce steam. The water was used in small quantities to keep the rocks from cooling too quickly. The sticks were taken from the holes and the holes plugged immediately.

A small fire was built on top of the covered pit and allowed to burn through the night.

Additional Resources

When selecting resources for studies of First Nations peoples, it is extremely important that the materials depict the people and the issues in an accurate, sensitive, and non-stereotypical way. A *Resource Reading List: Annotated Bibliography of Resources By and About Native People* produced by the Canadian Alliance in Solidarity with Native People provides the following guidelines to consider:

1. Does this book give insight into the values, the world view, the living vision of Native peoples?

2. Does this book lead to a deeper understanding and appreciation of Native cultures and Native peoples?

3. Does this book give insight into the diversity of Native cultures and Native peoples?

4. Are both sides of the events, issues, and differences provided?

5. Is information in this book accurate, misleading, or does it contain factual errors?

6. Is the image of the Native person(s) portrayed with human strengths and weaknesses, responding to his/her own nature and his/her own time?

7. Does the book acknowledge the contributions Native peoples have made to Western civilization?

8. Is this book sensitive to appropriate and accurate use of words and terminology (i.e., avoiding: chief, squaw, buck, Red skin, etc.)?

9. Would this book help a non-Native reader accept that "Indians are people like me"?

10. Would a Native reader be proud of this book and his/her heritage?

11. Does this book effectively counteract the negative stereotypes of Native peoples?

12. Has the book been reviewed by a person knowledgeable about Native peoples as well as the subject of the book?

13. Were Native people involved in the writing, illustration or publishing of the book?

14. What additional material is needed to give this book more relevance or to round it out?

15. How can this book best be used in a school curriculum to enhance a variety of themes, not only "Native studies"?

(Reproduced with Permission from the Canadian Alliance in Solidarity with Native Peoples.)

All of the materials included in this list have been recommended by the Canadian Alliance in Solidarity with Native Peoples or by First Nations consultants who were acknowledged at the opening of this Resource Guide.

Appreciation is extended to the Canadian Alliance in Solidarity with Native Peoples, who granted permission to copy some of these annotations from their Resource Reading List.

Resource (Print) Material Suggested for Elementary

Beaudry, L. Kawin. *A Book of Indian Crafts to Do*. Toronto, Ont.: Fitzhenry and Whiteside, 1975.
  An excellent book describing aboriginal crafts for children to make. Prepared in consultation with Native people.

Beavon, Daphne Odjig. *Legends of Nanabush*. Toronto, Ont.: Ginn Reading Series.
  Legends retold and illustrated by Ojibway artist Daphne Odjig.

Bellingham, Brenda. *Storm Child*. Toronto, Ont.: Lorimer, 1985.
  Isobel Macpherson is the 12-year-old daughter of a Scottish fur trader and a Peigan woman in the 1830s. She is torn between two very different lifestyles — one with her traditional Peigan grandparents, the other at the Hudson's Bay post.

Bemister, Margaret. *Thirty Indian Legends of Canada*. Vancouver, B.C.: Douglas and McIntyre, 1986.
  A good variety of legends from different Native cultures across Canada.

Blades, Ann. *A Boy of Tache*. Toronto, Ont.: Lorimer, 1980.
  Tache is an Indian reserve in northern British Columbia. This story of Charlie, Za, and Virginia is based on a true episode that occurred while Ann Blades was teaching there.

Blythe, A. *A Bit of Yesterday*. Winnipeg, Man.: Pemmican Publications, 1982.
  A collection of short stories that reflect a way of life on the prairies.

Brown, Vinson, and Phyllis Johnson, (Ed.). *Return of the Indian Spirit.* Berkeley, CA: Celestial Arts, 1981.
An aboriginal boy raised in the city learns from his grandmother the culture of his ancestors and discovers the pride of his people.

Cameron, Anne. *Dzelarhons: Myths of the Northwest Coast.* 1986.
Stories told to the author when she was a child by Klopinum, her Salish "auntie".

Cameron, Anne. *How Raven Freed the Moon.* 1985
Orca's Song. 1986
Raven Returns the Water. 1987
How the Loon Lost Her Voice. 1987
Lazy Boy. 1988. Madeira Park, B.C.: Harbour Publishing Co.
These five legends written, not by a Native author, but by a non-Native who grew up on the Northwest Coast, relate traditional tales of the peoples of the Coast.

Campbell, Maria. *Little Badger and the Fire Spirit.* Toronto, Ont.: McClelland & Stewart, 1980.
Stunningly illustrated in full color by David Maclagan. This superb book by a Métis author has profound meanings for all ages and lends itself to creative drama.

Cardinal, Phyllis, & Ripley, Dale. *Canada's People: The Métis.* Edmonton, Alta.: Plains Publishing, 1987.
Through discussions with his grandfather, a young Métis boy learns about his cultural heritage as a Métis.

Clark, Ella Elizabeth. *Indian Legends of Canada.* Toronto, Ont.: McClelland & Stewart, 1981.
Stories are arranged by theme and sometimes with introductory comments.

Cleaver, Elizabeth & Toye, William. *The Mountain Goats of Temlahem.* Toronto, Ont.: Oxford, 1969.
Stunning pictures illustrate this Tsimshian legend vividly teaching that greed leads to destruction and survival depends upon our respect for the natural world.

Clutesi, George. *Son of Raven, Son of Deer.* Vancouver, B.C.: Evergreen Press, 1967, 1975.
Fables of the Tse-Shaht people. Great collection of West Coast tales with an introduction to the role of oral "literature" in Native cultures.

Common, Diane. *Little Wild Onion of the Lillooet.* Winnipeg, Man.: Pemmican Publications, 1982.
Describes the daily life of a child and her people traveling along the Fraser Canyon. Two coyote stories show the Native values of compromise, fairness, and harmony.

Culleton B., *Spirit of the White Bison.* Winnipeg, Man.: Pemmican Publications, 1985.
The story of the mythical white buffalo who finds a kindred spirit in the man Lone Wolf. Told in the voice of the buffalo who will return from the spirit world to walk with those who are gentle and strong.

Dereume, A., & Zola, M. *Nobody.* Winnipeg, Man.: Pemmican Publications, 1984.
Nobody in a family of three mischievous youngsters is ever responsible for the pranks which drive mother frantic.

Dewdney, Selwyn. *The Hungry Time.* Toronto, Ont.: Lorimer, 1980.
This is the story of a Mississauga Indian girl named Morning Sky who, with her family, spends the winter camped at the mouth of the Humber River. Cold and hunger threaten their survival but, by facing these hardships together, a very special and powerful bond is created among the members of the family.

Dewdney, S. *They Shared to Survive: The Native Peoples of Canada*, Toronto, Ont.: Macmillan, 1975.
Description of the major cultural groups of Canada's First Peoples. Behind the book is the author's conviction that "there have been enduring contributions made by the first natives of this land" and "Canadians cannot afford to separate their interests from those of Native peoples: over the long term our needs and dangers are identical."

Evans, Hubert. *Son of the Salmon People.* Madeira Park, B.C.: Harbour Publishing Co., 1981.
Hal, returning from high school to his reserve on a B.C. salmon river, soon discovers where he stands in the struggle between human greed and the natural environment.

Fichter, George S. *How the Plains Indians Lived.* New York: David McKay Company, Inc., 1980.
Text and illustrations reveal the many-faceted lifestyle of over twenty North American tribes of the Great Plains.

Fox, Mary-Lou. *How the Bees Got their Stingers.* West Bay, Manitoulin Island: Ojibway Cultural Foundation, 1977.
Each creature, however big or small, has a purpose in life.

Fox, Mary-Lou. *Why the Beaver Has a Broad Tail.* Cobalt, B.C.: Highway Book Shop, 1984.
Another tale from the Ojibway, this one relates the story of the beaver's tail.

George, Dan. *My Heart Soars*. Vancouver, B.C.: Hancock Publishing, 1974.

George, Dan. *My Spirit Soars*. Vancouver, B.C.: Hancock Publishing, 1982.
Both Chief Dan George's books are collections of poetic and philosophical thoughts about the past and the future of his people, the Burrard Band of British Columbia.

Harris, Christie. *Raven's Cry*. Toronto, Ont.: McClelland & Stewart, 1966.
This fictionalized account of contact between the Haida and the Europeans describes the devastating effects of contact, as well as the attempts to preserve the rich Haida culture.

Hudson, Jan. *Sweetgrass*. Edmonton, Alta.: Tree Frog Press, 1984.
This is the story of a 15-year-old Blood Indian girl who learns about life and love during the early 19th century. Set in the historic horse-and-gun period of the Blackfoot confederacy, this novel won the 1984 CLA Book of the Year Award and the 1984 Canada Council Children's Literature Prize.

Jensen, D., & Sargent, P. *Robes of Power*. Vancouver, B.C.: UBC Press, 1986.
A Gitskan woman explains the history and meaning of the button blankets and describes how to make them.

Logie, Patricia, R. *Chronicles of Pride: Journey of Discovery*. Calgary, Alta.: Detselig, 1990.
Learn about the struggles and triumphs of fascinating and inspirational individuals from different First Nations. This is the account of the artist's experience meeting and painting the First Nations people who comprise the study. Colored reproductions of the 31 paintings are included.

McConkey, Lois. *Sea and Cedar: How the Northwest Coast Indians Lived*. Vancouver, B.C.: J.J. Douglas Ltd., 1973.
Northwest Coast native canoes, housing, food, clothing, tools, potlatches, beliefs and art are presented with easy to read text.

Okanagan Tribal Council. *How Names Were Given*. Penticton, B.C.: Theytus Books, 1984.
Teaches that everything on earth has been given a purpose, that real importance comes with responsibility to help others, and that even our failings can be turned to good.

Okanagan Tribal Council. *How Turtle Set the Animals Free*. Penticton, B.C.: Theytus Books, 1984.
This Okanagan Tale of how Turtle saves the animals from slavery, shows that good leadership depends on wisdom and vision rather than physical force.

Nowlan, Alden. *Nine Micmac Legends*. Hantsport, N.S.: Lancelot Press, 1983.
Illustrated by Shirley Bear, these stories teach values and ways of living.

Plouffe, V., Kissel, K., & Thompson, S. *The Winds of Change: Indian Government*. Edmonton, Alta.: Reidmore Books, 1988.
In a very easy-to-read style, this book introduces children to the ways of a reserve.

Santor, D.M. *Canada's Native People*. Scarborough, Ont.: Prentice-Hall, 1974.
Tells the story of the Indians, the Inuit, and the Métis, from the time of their first appearance in Canada to their current attempts to regain control of their own destiny. Includes contemporary photographs, pictures, and a variety of documents.

Scribe, M. *Murdo's Story: A legend from Northern Manitoba*. Winnipeg, Man.: Pemmican Publications, 1986.
This dramatic story, magnificently illustrated by Terry Gallagher, dramatizes the way of survival for us all through creative thinking, cooperation, and negotiation.

Sharp, Edith. *Nkwala*. Toronto, Ont.: McClelland & Stewart, 1984.
This meticulously researched story about a Pokan boy's spirit quest (set in southern Okanagan) provides detailed insight into the culture of the Interior Salish.

Sliammon Indian Band Stories. *Mink and Cloud. Mink and Grey Bird*. Cloverdale, B.C.: D.W. Friesen & Sons Ltd, 1985.
These Northwest Coast legends are illustrated with traditional Northwest Coast black, white and red images.

Smucker, Barbara. *White Mist*. Toronto, Ont.: Irwin Publishing, 1985.
An adopted Native girl and a boy from the reserve, discover their roots and traditional values: "If we destroy the earth, we destroy ourselves. We are one with the earth."

Steltzer, Ulli. *A Haida Potlatch*. Vancouver, B.C.: Douglas & McIntyre, 1984.
This book is a visual celebration of a potlatch given in Masset by Haida artist Robert Davidson, to mark the adoption of his fellow artist-brother and to invite the whole village to give names in the traditional way.

Stewart, Hilary. *Cedar*. Vancouver, B.C.: Douglas & McIntyre, 1984.
This book provides a superb explanation of the basic technologies and products of the cedar tree. Indexed.

Stewart, Hilary. *Indian Fishing*. Vancouver, B.C.: J.J. Douglas Ltd., 1977.
Fish was the basis of the Northwest Coast Native diet. The types of fish and methods for catching and preparing the fish are presented in this well illustrated book.

Thompson, Sheila & Steele, Louise. *The Spirit of the Coast Salish*. Vancouver, B.C.: Creative Curriculum Inc., 1987.
An easy-to-read format and informative narrative of the traditional ways of the Coast Salish.

Waterton, Betty. *A Salmon for Simon*. Vancouver, B.C.: Douglas & McIntyre, 1978.
Simon lives in a village on the west coast. All summer he has been fishing for salmon but encounters the frustrations of any small boy. His luck changes when an eagle carrying a salmon in its claws accidentally drops it into a tidal pool. He is torn between sympathy for the fish and a desire to catch something of his own.

Weir, Joan. *So, I'm Different*. Vancouver, B.C.: Douglas & McIntyre, 1981.
Nicky has had a hard time — he moved to a new house and school, his dog got run over, and worst of all, his teacher singles him out because he is the only Indian in the school.

Resource (Print) Material Suggested for Secondary and Teacher Background

Alexander, H.B. *World's Rim*. Lincoln, NB.: University of Nebraska Press, 1958.
Great mysteries of the North American Indian.

Armstrong, Jeanette. *Slash*. Penticton, B.C.: Theytus Books, 1986.
A fictional story of a young man's journey from childhood in a traditional Okanagan home through confusion, prison, political activism and finally a spiritual at-homeness.

Barbeau, Marius. *Art of the Totem*. Surrey, B.C.: Hancock House, revised 1984.
A valuable book about the carving of totems and their roles in Northwest Coast cultures. First published in 1932, the book was revised and published again in 1984.

Barman, Jean, Yvonne Hebert & Don McCaskill (eds.). *Indian Education in Canada*. Vancouver, B.C.: University of British Columbia, 1986.
Eight essays written by Native and non-Native scholars and teachers from across Canada. Argues for Indian control of education.

Brown, Vinson. *Great Upon the Mountain.* New York: Macmillan, 1971.
Referred to by Yvonne Dunlop, this book explores cultural and spiritual values and concepts of First Nations peoples.

Brown, Vinson. *Voices of Earth and Sky.* Happy Valley, CA.: Naturegraph, 1974.
Referred to by Yvonne Dunlop, this book explores cultural and spiritual values and concepts of First Nations peoples.

Burger, Julian. *Report from the Frontier: The State of the World's Indigenous Peoples.* Atlantic Highlands, NJ: Humanities Press Int., 1987.
Examines the situation of Indigenous peoples whose vulnerable and exploited communities exist in half the countries of the world. Documents their health, employment, educational disadvantages, sources of conflict with government and multinationals and their growing resistance.

Brody, Hugh. *Maps and Dreams.* Vancouver, B.C.: Douglas & McIntyre, 1981
The author vividly describes a year in the vibrant culture of the Beaver in northeastern British Columbia.

Cameron, Anne. *Daughters of Copper Woman.* Vancouver, B.C.: Press Gang Publishers, 1981.
Oral tradition told to the author by women of an ancient society on Vancouver Island.

Campbell, Maria. *Riel's People: How the Métis Lived.* Vancouver, B.C.: Douglas & McIntyre, 1987.
Illustrated by David Maclagan, this book expresses both the pride and the isolation of the author's people.

Campbell, Maria. *People of the Buffalo: How the Plains Indians Lived.* Vancouver, B.C.: Douglas & McIntyre, 1976
The Author's account of the traditional lives of the Natives of the Plains.

Clutesi, George. *Son of Raven, Son of Deer.* Vancouver, B.C.: Evergreen Press, 1967.
Fables of the Tse-Shaht people. Great collection of West Coast tales with an introduction to the role of oral "literature" in Native cultures.

Craven, Margaret. *I Heard the Owl Call My Name.* Toronto, Ont.: Irwin Publishing, 1967.
The story of a terminally ill Anglican minister who lived with the Kwakiutl on the central B.C. coast. A look at Native culture.

Crowe, K.J. *A History of the Original Peoples of Northern Canada*. Toronto, Ont.: McGill/Queens University Press, 1974.
Told from a Native viewpoint.

Deloria, Vine, Jr. *Indians of the Pacific Northwest Coast*. Toronto, Ont.: Doubleday of Canada, 1977.
An excellent account of the history of coastal Natives to contemporary times.

DeTremaudan, A.H. *Hold High Your Heads*. Winnipeg, Man.: Pemmican Publications, 1986.
History of the Métis Nation in Western Canada.

Dewdney, S. *They Shared to Survive*: *The Native Peoples of Canada*. Toronto, Ont.: Macmillan, 1975.
Description of the major cultural groups of Canada's First People. Behind the book is the author's conviction that "there have been enduring contributions made by the first natives of this land" and "Canadians cannot afford to separate their interests from those of Native peoples: over the long term our needs and dangers are identical."

Duffek, K. *Bill Reid*: *Beyond the Essential Form*. Vancouver, B.C.: UBC Press, 1986.
An easy-to-follow discussion of Bill Reid's life and work and its relation to other Haida art. Shows the importance of Native art to the increasing public awareness of Native values.

Dyck, Noel (ed.) *Indigenous Peoples and the Nation State*. Ottawa: Institute for Social and Economic Research, 1985.
Examines fourth world politics in Canada, Australia and Norway.

Fisher, R. *Contact and Conflict*. Vancouver, B.C.: UBC Press, 1977.
Indian-European relations in British Columbia at the time of initial contact. Challenges the patronizing interpretation of many histories of the time.

Friederes, J.S. *Native Peoples in Canada: Contemporary Conflicts*. (Second Edition). Scarborough, Ont.: Prentice-Hall, 1983.
Covers treaties, claims, population distribution, urban Native peoples, policies of government and Native organizations.

Goodwill, J., & Sluman, N. *John Tootoosis*. Winnipeg, Man.: Pemmican Publications, 1984.
Awarded the Order of Canada in 1986, John Tootoosis is a remarkable man and a symbol of strength and leadership. This book, written by his daughter, traces the history of Tootoosis' people going back to treaty number 6.

Harris, Christie. *Raven's Cry*. Toronto, Ont.: McClelland & Stewart, 1966.
This fictionalized account of contact between the Haida and the Europeans describes the devastating effects of contact, as well as the attempts to preserve the rich Haida culture.

Harris, Christie. *Sky Man On the Totem Pole*. Toronto, Ont.: McClelland, 1975.
A gripping and mind-stretching fantasy based on the stories of the Temlahem from the Northwest Coast.

Hays, H.E. *Children of the Raven: The Seven Indian Nations of the Northwest Coast*. Toronto, Ont.: McGraw-Hill, 1975.
In the words of the author: "It seems to me that a society such as ours, which has formed its values on the acquisition, retention, control, and manipulation of wealth, has something to learn from a people which gains social approval by giving it away."

Kirk, Ruth. *Wisdom of the Elders*: Native Traditions on the Northwest Coast. Vancouver, B.C.: Douglas & McIntyre, 1986.
Native traditions of the past are described, including those of kinship, rank, trade, religion, and daily life. (Indexed).

Laurence, M. *In Search of April Raintree*. Winnipeg, Man.: Pemmican Publications, 1983.
A novel concerning the treatment of Métis children in white foster homes.

Logie, Patricia, R. *Chronicles of Pride: Journey of Discovery*. Calgary, Alta.: Detselig, 1990.
Learn about the struggles and triumphs of fascinating and inspirational individuals from different First Nations. This is the account of the artist's experience meeting and painting the First Nations people who comprise the study. Colored reproductions of the 31 paintings are included.

Lowes, Warren. *Indian Giver: A Legacy of North American Native Peoples*. Penticton, B.C.: Theytus Books, 1986.
The myriad contributions of Native peoples to our present society, including language, survival skills, sports, healing, agriculture, government, and a vision for survival tomorrow.

Manuel, George. *Fourth World: An Indian Reality*. Toronto, Ont.: Collier McMillan, 1974.
In this book George Manuel explores the place of Indigenous people in the contemporary world.

McLuhan, T.C. *Touch the Earth*: An Indian Self Portrait. New York: Promontory Books, 1975.
A collection of oral literature from Native people of the past. Impressive for dignity and wisdom. Should be balanced with a contemporary voice.

McMillan, Alan D. *Native Peoples and Cultures of Canada.* Vancouver, B.C.: Douglas & McIntyre, 1988.
An up-to-date view of Canadian Native peoples, past and present. McMillan, an anthropologist rejoices in the resurgence of Native identity. The book misses important cultural contexts such as the philosophical and spiritual aspects of First Nations peoples.

Native Indian Brotherhood. *Indian Control of Indian Education.* Policy Paper, Ottawa, Ont. 1975.

Okanagan Tribal Council. *How Food Was Given.* Penticton, B.C.: Theytus Books, 1984.
This moving story illuminates the basic and universal Native value — human relationship with the animal and plant world must be one of interdependence and respect.

Okanagan Tribal Council. *How Turtle Set the Animals Free.* Penticton, B.C.: Theytus Books, 1984.
This Okanagan Tale of how Turtle saves the animals from slavery, shows that good leadership depends on wisdom and vision rather than physical force.

Raunet, Daniel. *Without Surrender, Without Consent: A History of Nisga'a Land Claims.* Vancouver, B.C.: Douglas & McIntyre, 1984.

Ryga, George. *Ecstasy of Rita Joe.* Don Mills, Ont.: New Press, 1971.
Ryga's powerful play about a young British Columbia woman caught in a web of societal forces beyond her control or understanding.

Sharp, Edith. *Nkwala.* Toronto, Ont.: McClelland & Stewart, 1984.
This meticulously researched story about a Pokan boy's spirit quest (set in southern Okanagan) provides a detailed insight into the culture of the Interior Salish.

Silko, Leslie Marmon. *Storytelling.* New York: Seaver Books, 1981.
Uses Native oral traditions to express feelings and thoughts of Native life, past and present.

Storm, Hyemeyohsts. *Seven Arrows.* New York: Ballantine Books, 1985.
Referred to by Yvonne Dunlop, this book explores cultural and spiritual values and concepts of First Nations peoples.

Titley, E. Brian. *A Narrow Vision: Duncan Campbell Scott and the Administration of Indian Affairs in Canada.* Vancouver, B.C.: UBC Press, 1986.
Shows how history creates the present. A scathing exposé of government policies and the Department of Indian Affairs.

University of Victoria. *Aboriginal Title, Rights, and the Constitution: Proceeding of the 1983 Symposium.* Victoria, B.C.: University of Victoria, 1985.
Speeches made by Native leaders explaining their position on Aboriginal rights.

Willoya, William and Brown, Vinson. *Warriors of the Rainbow: Strange and Prophetic Dreams of Indian Peoples.* Happy Valley, CA: Naturegraph, 1962.
Referred to by Yvonne Dunlop, this book explores cultural and spiritual values and concepts of First Nations peoples.

Woodcock, George. *Peoples of the Coast*: *The Indians of the Pacific Northwest.* Edmonton, Alta.: Hurtig Press, 1977.
This is an intriguing, well illustrated description of the Native cultures. (Indexed).

Teaching Resources

Curriculum

British Columbia Teachers' Federation. *To Potlatch or Not to Potlatch*. Lesson Aids #2011. (BCTF Lesson Aids, 2235 Burrard St., Vancouver, B.C., V6J 3J9)
Available through the BCTF, this resource has copies of letters and articles from newspapers from the time of the banning of the potlatch on the West Coast. Includes information from both government officials and the Native peoples and encourages students to consider the positions taken.

Caduto, Michael, and Bruchat, Joseph. *Keepers of the Earth: North American Stories and Environmental Activities for Children.* Boston: University Press, 1990.
Detailed lessons in science and environmental studies are related to traditional stories and wisdom.

Conner, Daniel and Bethune, Doreen. *UBC Curriculum Research Project: Native People and Explorers of Canada.* Toronto, Ont.: Prentice-Hall, 1984.
Student text. Many attractive illustrations, word check list, questions for discussion and investigation. Two children, the author and the elders tell about their lives in their communities: "Our Arctic Way of Life", and "Our Coast Salish Way of Life". Also chapters on the Nuu-chah-nulth, people of the Eastern Woodlands, and people of the Plains.

Cooper, Amy Jo. *Dream Quest.* Toronto, Ont.: Annik Press & Gagne Printing Ltd.
Part of Spirit Bay Series. Annex Jr. Language Art Kits. Contains 6 copies of one title, teacher's guide, laminated student activity cards.

First Nations House of Learning (1990-91). First Nations Studies.
A calendar of courses available for Native students at University of British Columbia. For copies of the calendar contact the First Nations House of Learning. It also includes a Directory of Vancouver agencies for First Nations.

Kirkness, Verna. *Indians of the Plains.* Toronto, Ont.: Grollier, 1984.
Includes ideas and values, traditional ways and contemporary life, historic and modern illustrations, words to know, thinking and doing activities.

L'ilawat. National Film Board of Canada and Department of Indian and Northern Affairs, Ottawa, Ont: 1982.
A kit containing slides, recordings of Salishan language, filmstrips, toys, charts and photographs. The story of the L'ilawat Nation is told from their perspective.

MacLean, Hope. *Indians, Inuit, and Métis of Canada.* Toronto, Ont.: Gage, 1982.
A clear and reasonably accurate story of Native peoples of Canada focusing on the seven major groups, including some contemporary issues. Based on a kit published by the Canadian Association in Support of Native People.

Queen Charlotte Island Reading Series. Vancouver, B.C.: Wedge, 1984.
This series of twelve student books includes legends, stories, and information about the Haida people. Aimed at primary school-age students, reading levels are marked "A" for easy; "B" for medium; "C" for harder. The booklets range from twenty-two to twenty-four pages. A Teacher's Guide is included with the series.

Sacred Tree, The. Four Worlds Development Press, University of Lethbridge, Lethbridge, Alta.: 1986
Curriculum package includes videos. The text is beautifully illustrated and presents the universal concepts and teachings handed down in Native cultures.

Verrall, Catherine. *All My Relations.* Toronto, Ont.: Canadian Alliance in Solidarity with the Native Peoples, 1987.
A kit for teachers and group leaders of elementary school-aged students. Ways to discover living values through stories, drama, poetry, art, symbols, music, games, and projects.

Verrall, Catherine and McDowell, Patricia in consultation with Lenore Keeshig-Tobias. *Resource Reading List: Annotated Bibliography of Resources by and about Native People.* Toronto, Ont.: Canadian Alliance in Solidarity with the Native Peoples, 1990.
An excellent annotated bibliography of materials and resources for and about Native Peoples.

Films and Videos

Augusta. National Film Board of Canada, 16 min., 1976.
A delightful 88-year-old grandmother of the Shuswap shares her stories and her kindness, her harmonica and her sense of humor. Support material.

Bill Reid. NFB, 28 min., 1979.
The artist's account of his work and the raising of the pole at Skidegate in a Haida ceremony.

Berger Inquiry, The. Distributor: Native Communications Group, 30 min, 1976.
The information given to the McKenzie Valley Pipeline Inquiry by the Inuit and Dene people on the value of land to Native people, has a wide application to the whole question of land claims and cultural traditions.

Box of Treasures. Campus Film Distributors Corporation (CFDC), 30 min, 1983.
In the late 19th century, the Canadian government removed ritual objects from the possession of the Kwakiutl. In 1980, at Alert Bay, the U'Mista Cultural Centre opened its doors to receive and house the cultural treasures which had been seized decades earlier. This film documents the cultural significance of these events.

Chronicles of Pride. United Native Nations, 20 min, 1990.
This film includes interviews of five of the subjects in the series, or their families: Blanche Macdonald, Gloria George, Mildred Gottfriedson, Judge Alfred Scow, and Vivian Wilson. The video tells each of their stories and introduces important issues.

Cold Journey. National Film Board (NFB), 75 min, 1972.
Based on the tragic and true story of an Indian boy's search for meaning, the cultural shock and cruelty of the white man's education system, and the resulting despair.

Colours of Pride, The. Canadian Department of Indian and Northern Affairs (CDIAND) 27 min, 1973.
Introduces the work and values of four Native artists: Norval Morrisseau, Allen Sapp, Daphne Odjig, and Alex Janvier.

Dancing Around the Table. NFB, 1989.
In two parts, this production looks at the events of the four constitutional conferences between the federal and provincial governments, and the Native peoples of Canada. The film covers the conferences in detail with actual debate shown. It is interspersed with remembrances of Ethel Pearson, an elder of the Kwakiutl Nation.

Daughters of the Country. NFB, 1986.
In a four part series, the struggle of the Métis is dramatized, showing that in many ways they are caught between two worlds.

Great Spirit, The. NFB, 27 min.
Many Native people are finding new strength in their traditional religious ways. This film shows a rare glimpse of their sacred places and ceremonies. Includes a discussion with Ernest Tootoosis.

I Was Born Here. Distributor: CDIAND, 1976.
A moving tribute to the intense feeling of relationship between the people and the land. Presents the Dene people of the Mackenzie Valley.

Journey to Strength. Leonard George, Dan George Memorial Foundation, Thomas Howe Association, Vancouver, B.C., 1987
Documents the successes of B.C. bands and Native organizations and highlights Native concerns in education, health, fishing, culture, and government.

Kevin Alex. NFB, 16 min, 1976.
Near Lillooet, B.C., 11-year-old Kevin learns traditional skills and family values. Support material available.

Last Mooseskin Boat, The. NFB, 28 min, 1982.
This documentary records the passing of a tradition of the Shotah Dene of the Northwest Territories. Gabe Etchinelle returns to the mountains of his youth to build one last mooseskin boat, which is now preserved in the museum in Yellowknife.

Legend of Magic Knives. Encyclopedia Britannica Educational Films, 11 min, 1971.
This Northwest Coast legend recounts the story of an old chief who realizes his apprentice's carvings are better than his own. He attempts to strike the guardian of the carvings, but kills himself instead. In death, he chooses to be a river, flowing close to his native tribe. The film covers the importance of totem poles, their figures and their creation by a carver.

Man, the Snake, and the Fox, The. NFB, 11 min, 1978.
Basil Johnston tells a traditional Ojibway legend to Native children. This moving story enacted with impressive masks, could lead to a discussion about keeping your promises.

Moon Mask, by Freda Diesing. CDIAND, 10 min, 1977.
A modern Haida artist carves and decorates a moon mask with skill and pride.

Ninstints: Shadow Keepers of the Past. CFDC, 30 min, 1983.
The story of the abandoned Haida village of Ninstints on remote Anthony Island off the tip of the Queen Charlottes. Footage takes the village from its height, to the removal of some totem poles to museums, up to today's conservation program of the B.C. Provincial Museum.

Other Side of the Ledger, The: An Indian View of the Hudson's Bay Company. NFB, 43 min; 18 min, abridged, 1972.
Contemporary Native spokesmen present the Native people's perspective about Hudson's Bay Company operations.

Our Land is Our Life. NFB, 57 min, 1974.
A powerful presentation of the effects of the James Bay Power Project on the Cree, before the James Bay Agreement.

Our Totem is the Raven. Holt Reinhart, 21 min, 1972.
Chief Dan George takes a 15-year-old urban Native boy into the bush to explain the ways of his forefathers in a meaningful way.

Potlatch: A Strict Law Bids Us Dance., 53 min, CDIAND, 1975.
This film traces the history of conflict between European settlers and Native peoples. It emphasizes the outlawing of the potlatch and the trials and confiscation of ceremonial objects which occurred in 1922. The film provides a sensitive look at a clash of values and this can be applied to the mid- and late-nineteenth century as well.

Rediscovery: The Eagle's Gift. CFDC, 29 min, 1984.
   On a remote island off the northwest coast of British Columbia, is the most isolated wilderness camp in the world. Here Native and non-Native youngsters embark on a journey of self wonder and discover the Haida culture of the Queen Charlotte Islands.

Salmon People. NFB, 25 min, 1977.
   Contrasts the traditional relationship of Native people to the salmon, with modern fishing practices. The legend is a warning for us all today: respect the environment or perish.

Somewhere Between, CFD, 50 min, 1982.
   The controversy surrounding laws which discriminate against Native women unfolds against the background of the personal experiences of five women in British Columbia. The film reveals the alienation of these women when they are forced to live apart from their communities because of the change in their legal status under the Indian Act.

Survival in the Bush. NFB, 30 min, 1954.
   A look at how two men survive in the bush with only an axe. One man, a Canadian Forces pilot, is totally dependent on the other, a Cree, for survival.

Totem Poles. Indiana University, 27 min, (color), 1961.
   The significance and symbolism of seven types of Northwest Coast poles and house posts are described and illustrated, as are the steps in carving a pole.

Treaty 8 Country, CFD, 44 min, 1982.
   Hunting as a way of life for Native people is threatened by large-scale resource development. The film reveals their world through the detail of daily life in a summer hunting camp.

Music and Sound Recordings

The Drums of Poundmaker. 1977. Canyon, C 6156-6157.
   Two disks. Tootoosis Family.

Indian Music of the Pacific Northwest Coast. 1974. Folkways, FE 4523.
   Collected and recorded by Ida Halpern. Brochure notes, 36 pp.

Davies, Sandra and Joan Buchanan. *Music in Our Lives: The Pacific Northwest Coast Indians*. Vancouver, B.C.: Wedge, UBC, 1980.
Music, instruments, legends. Includes a booklet, a cassette, and 24 slides.

Indian Music of the Canadian Plains. 1955. Folkways, FE 4464. Recorded by Kenneth Peacock.
Inuit Traditional Songs and Games. Distributed by Boots Records. SQN 108. Collected in Northern Quebec; includes booklet in English, French and Inuktitut.

Iroquois Social Dances Songs. 1969. Iroquois Crafts, QC 727-729.
Three discs plus brochure notes by William Guy Spittal.

Native Storytelling. Manitoba Education Branch, 40 min, 1982.
Weskachak legends are told by Native storyteller Ron Roulet. The role of storytelling in traditional culture is explained.

People of the Salmon. Written by David Campbell. Vancouver School Board, 1986.
Cassette and teacher's guide.

Language

Alison, R.M. *Mammal and Bird Names in the Indian Languages of Ontario*. Toronto, Ont.: Ontario Ministry of Natural Resources, 1986.

Frantz, Donald and Russell, Norma Jean. *The Blackfoot Dictionary of Stems, Roots and Affixes*. Toronto, Ont.: University of Toronto, 1988.

National Film Board of Canada and Department of Indian and Northern Affairs. *L'ilawat*. Ottawa, Ont.: CDIAND, 1982.

Manitoba Department of Education, Native Education Branch. *How to Learn to Read and Write Cree Syllabics* (Student Handbooks and Teacher's Edition). Winnipeg, Man.: Manitoba Department of Education, 1987.

Nichols, John (ed.) *An Ojibway Text Anthology*. Ottawa, Ont.: Centre for Research and Teaching Canadian Native Languages, 1988.

Shkilnyk, Anastasia. *Progress Report: Aboriginal Language Policy Development*, Brantford, Ont.: Woodland Indian Cultural Educational Centre, 1985.

Squamish Nation Education Department. *In the Long Ago (A Language Program)*. North Vancouver, B.C.: Quest Printing, 1987.

Witeskuk nikmaq aqq nitapq (Meet My Family and Friends): Teaching Kit for Micmac as a Second Language. Truro, N.S.: Native Council of Nova Scotia, 1987.

Wolfart, H. C. and Carroll, J. *Meet Cree: A Guide to the Cree Language*. Edmonton, Alta.: University of Alberta, 1981.

Woodland Indian Cultural Educational Centre. *English-Mohawk Lexicon: A Spelling Wordlist of Six Nations Mohawk*. Brantford, Ont.: Woodlands Indian Cultural Educational Centre, 1986.

Art and Artifacts

Barbeau, M. *Art of the Totem*. Surrey, B.C.: Hancock House, revised 1984.
A valuable book about the carving of totems and their roles in Northwest Coast cultures. First published in 1932, the book was revised and published again in 1984.

Coe, R. *Lost and Found Traditions: Native American Art 1965-1985*. Seattle, WA.: University of Washington Press, 1986.
Covers both Canada and the United States, traditional and contemporary art.

Dewdney, S. and Kidd, K. *Indian Rock Painting of the Great Lakes*. Toronto, Ont.: University of Toronto Press, 1962.
Native rock carvings of northern Ontario and Minnesota.

Dinniwell, N. and Hill, T. *From Masks to Maquettes*. Ottawa, Ont.: Department of Indian and Northern Affairs, 1985.
Catalogue of Iroquoian artists who have molded particular Iroquois traditions into a twentieth century international art form. Includes a clear photograph of each artist and each work as well as illuminating discussion.

Highwater, J. *The Sweet Grass Lives On: Fifty Contemporary North American Indian Artists.* Toronto, Ont.: Fitzhenry & Whiteside, 1980.
Includes information about the art and the lives of the artists.

Macduff, A. *Lords of the Stone.* Toronto, Ont.: Fitzhenry & Whiteside, 1980.
Contemporary Inuit sculptures, including full-color photographs. The text attempts to reveal the physical and spiritual characteristics of Inuit art, with information about each artist.

Johnson, E. L. & Bernick, K. *Hands of our Ancestors: The Revival of Salish Weaving at Musqueam.* Vancouver, B.C.: University of British Columbia Museum of Anthropology, 1986.

Steltzer, U. *Indian Artists at Work.* Vancouver, B.C.: J.J. Douglas Ltd., 1976.
A sensitive photographer visits artists of the Pacific Northwest.

Stewart, H. *Looking at Indian Art of the Northwest Coast.* Vancouver, B.C.: Douglas & McIntyre, 1979.
An excellent introduction to the technique , components, and designs of west coast art. Uses dozens of prints from major contemporary artists to systematically explain elements and theory of the art from.

Food and Medicines

Grimm, William. *Indian Harvests.* Toronto, Ont.: McGraw-Hill, 1973.
Describes important food uses of common wild plants in a readable style for young people.

McKechnie, Robert E. *Strong Medicine: A History of Healing on the Northwest Coast.* Vancouver, B.C.: Douglas & McIntyre, 1975.
The author takes special notice of the role of Indian curing traditions in the overall development of European knowledge. Dr. McKechnie devotes a number of chapters to the spiritual nature of Indian Healing.

People of K'san. *Gathering What the Great Nature Provided. Food traditions of the Gitksan.* Vancouver, B.C.: Douglas & McIntyre, 1980.
Includes photographs of the people today, tips for cooking, and a discussion of how food shaped the way of the Gitksan.

Turner, Nancy J., Bouchard, Randy, & Kennedy, Dorothy I.D. *Ethnobotany of the Okanagan. Colville Indians of British Columbia and Washington.* Occasional Paper Series #21. Victoria, B.C.: British Columbia Provincial Museum, 1980.

Aboriginal Voice
Ont. Métis & Aboriginal Assn.
158 Sackville Rd.
Sault Ste. Marie, ON
P6B 4T6
(705) 949-5161

**Aboriginal Women's
Council of Saskatchewan**
62-17th St. West
Prince Albert, SK
S6V 3X3

AFN Bulletin
Assembly of First Nations
47 Clarence St., Suite 300
Ottawa, ON
K1N 9K1

**AFN Education
Secretariat Newsletter**
Assembly of First Nations
47 Clarence St., Suite 300
Ottawa, ON
K1N 9K1 (free)

Agenutemagen
Union of New Brunswick Indians
35 Dedam St.
Fredricton, NB
E3B 3L6

Akwesasne Notes
Akwesasne Notes, Mohawk Nation
Box 196
Rooseveltown, NY
13683, US
BM $15

Alberta Native News
421, 10010-105 St.
Edmonton, AB
T5J 1C4
$25/yr

Alliance
La voix des métis et
Indiens sans statut du Quebec.
The voice of the Metis and
non-status Indians in Quebec
Native Alliance of Quebec
21 rue Brodeur
Hull, PQ
J8Y 2O6 8x/yr $10

Awasis Cree Child Journal
Indian and Native
Education Council
Box 1108
Saskatoon, SK
S7K 3N3, $10

**Dakota Ojibway Tribal Council
News**
Box 1148, 702 Douglas St.
Brandon, MN
R7A 6A4

**Dan Sha News (Yukon Indian
News)**
Ye Sa To Communications Society
22 Nisutlin Dr.
Whitehorse, YK
Y1A 4J5

Daybreak
Box 315
Williamsville, NY
14231, US Q $12

Eagle
Eagle Wing Press
Box 579 MO
Naugatuck, CT
06770, US
BM 28 page tabloid journal
by the American Indians of New
England

Four Winds
Hundred Arrows Press
Box 156
Austin, TX
78767, US Q $22

Ha-Shilth-Sa
Box 1255
Port Alberni, BC

**Indian and Inuit Nurses
of Canada Newsletter**
Indian and Inuit Nurses of Canada
47 Clarence St., 3rd flr.
Ottawa, Ont.
K1N 9K1 (free)

Indian Voice
Canadian Indian Voice Society
429 E 6th St.
N Vancouver, BC
V7C 1P8 Q $6.50

Indian World Magazine
Union of British Columbia Indian
Chiefs
73 Water St. #200
Vancouver, BC
Z6B 1A1

Inuktitut
Cultural and Linguistics Section
Northern Program
Indian and Northern Affairs
Ottawa, ON
K1A 0H4
In English and Inuktitut (free)

Journal of Indigenous Studies
Gabriel Dumont Institute
121 Broadway Ave. East
Regina, SK
S4N 0Z6
semi-annual, $20 annually ($30 for
institutions)

Kahtou
302-873 Beatty St.
Vancouver, BC
V6B 2M6

Kainai News
Indian News Media
Box 808
Cardston, AB

Mal-l-Mic News
New Brunswick Association of Métis
and non-status Indians
390 King St., Suite 1
Fredricton, NB

Messenger
William Head Institute
Indian Education Club
Box 10
Metochosin, BC

Métis Newsletter
Métis Association of the NWT
 Box 1375
Yellowknife, NWT
X1A 2P1

Le Métis
620-504 Main St.
Winnipeg, MN
R3B 1B8

Micmac News
Native Communications
Society of Nova Scotia
Box 344
Sydney, NS
B1P 6H2 BM $5

Native Network News
120-12520 St. Albert Trail
Edmonton, AB
T5L 4H4

Native Press
Native Communications
Society of Western NWT
Box 1919
Yellowknife, NWT
X1A 2P4

NATIVEscene
Native Media Network
Box 848
Portage La Prairie, MN
R1N 3C3

New Breed
Saskatchewan Native
Communications Corp.
210-2505 11th Ave.
Regina, SK
S4P 0K6

Nunatsiaq News
P.O. Box 8
Iquluit NWT
X0A 0H0
(819) 979-5357
English & Inuktitut

Ontario Indian
Union of Ontario Indians
27 Queen St. E. 2nd flr.
Toronto, ON
M5C 2M6 M $10

**Ontario Native Women's
Association Newsletter**
278 Bay St.
Thunder Bay, ON

Phoenix
Canadian Alliance in Solidarity
with Native Peoples
Box 574 Stn. P
Toronto, ON
M5S 2T1
seasonally. free to members

**SAFC & Justice
Service Letter**
Sask. Association of
Friendship Centres
225-22nd St. East
Saskatoon, SK
S7K 0G4

**Sans Reserve: Expressions Auto-
chtones d'ici et d'aujourd'hui
Communications Autochtones**
3575 boul St. Laurent, Suite 513
Montreal, PQ
H2X 2T7

Saskatchewan Indian
Sask. Indian Media Corp
107, 2103 Airport Dr.
Saskatoon, SK
S7L 6WA M $15

Saskatchewan Indian Federated College, Journal
College W. Bldg. #127
Regina, SK
S4S 0A2

Suvaguuq—Inuit Women's Association Newsletter
200 Elgin St., #804
Ottawa, ON
K2P 1L5
(613) 234-3988

Taqralik
Makivik Corporation
Box 179
Kuujjuaq, PQ
J0M 1C0

Tekawennake
Box 130
Ohsweken, ON
N0A 1M0

Tekawennake Six Nations-New Credit Reporter
Woodland Indian Cultural-Educational Centre
184 Mohawk St., Box 1506
Brantford, ON
N3T 5V6

Theata
University of Alaska
Alaska Native Programs
Fairbanks, AK
9970, US A $5

Turtle
Native American Centre
for the Living Arts
25 Rainbow Mall
Niagara Falls, NY
14303, U.S.
Quarterly, $15 in Canada,
$10 U.S.

Tuskaayakst
Western Arctic Inuit
Box 1704
Inuvik, NWT
X0E 0T0 (403) 979-2320

Vision Quest
4288 Welwyn St.
Vancouver, BC
V5N 3Z4

Wawatay News
34 Front St.
Box 1180
Sioux Lookout, ON
P0V 2T0

Western Native News
#907, 626 West Pender
Vancouver, BC
V6B 1V9

Windspeaker
Aboriginal Multi-Media
Society of Alberta
15001-112th Ave.
Edmonton, AB
T5M 2V6 BW $26

Yorkton District Tribal Newsletter
54 Smith St. West
Yorkton, SK
S3N 0J1

Maps

Tribes And Native Language Families of Canada

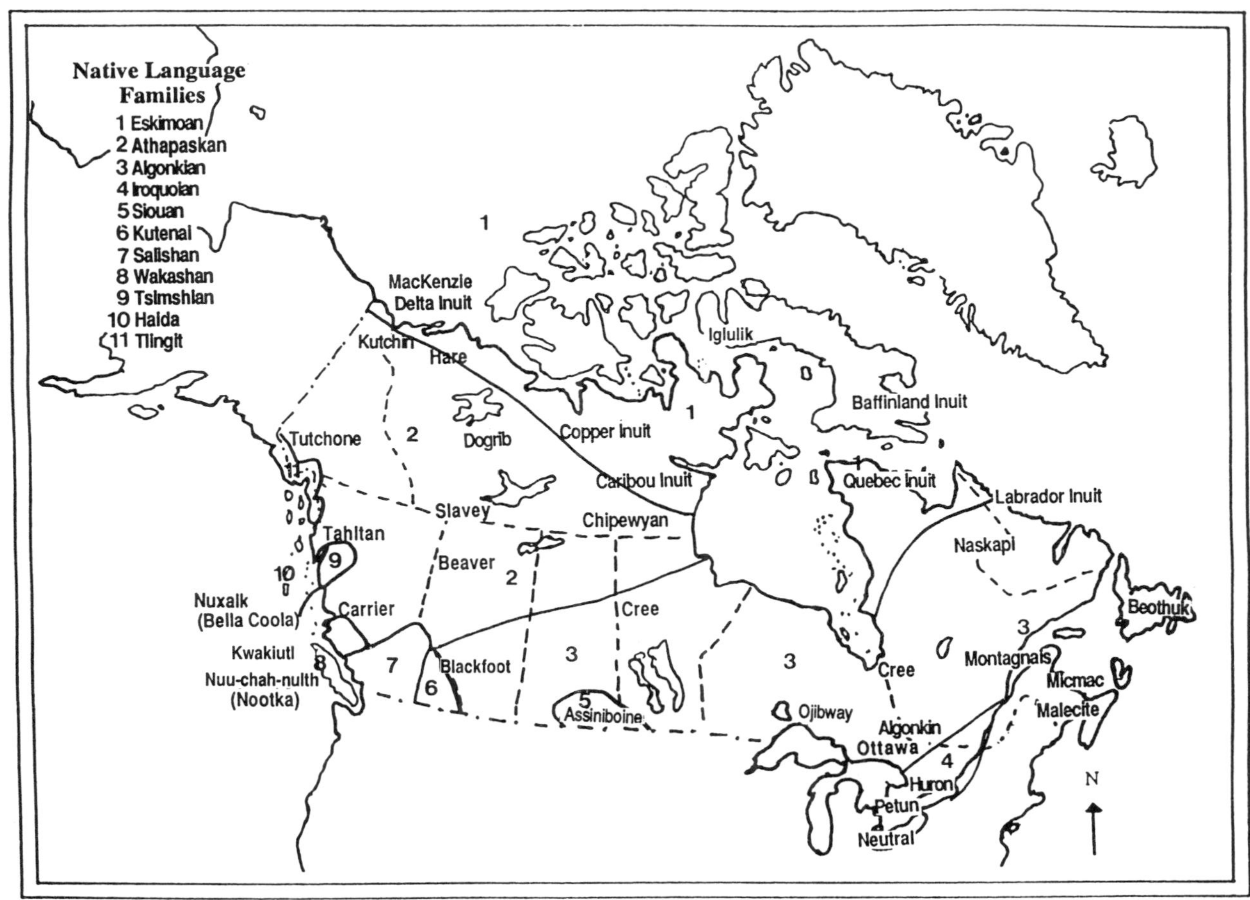

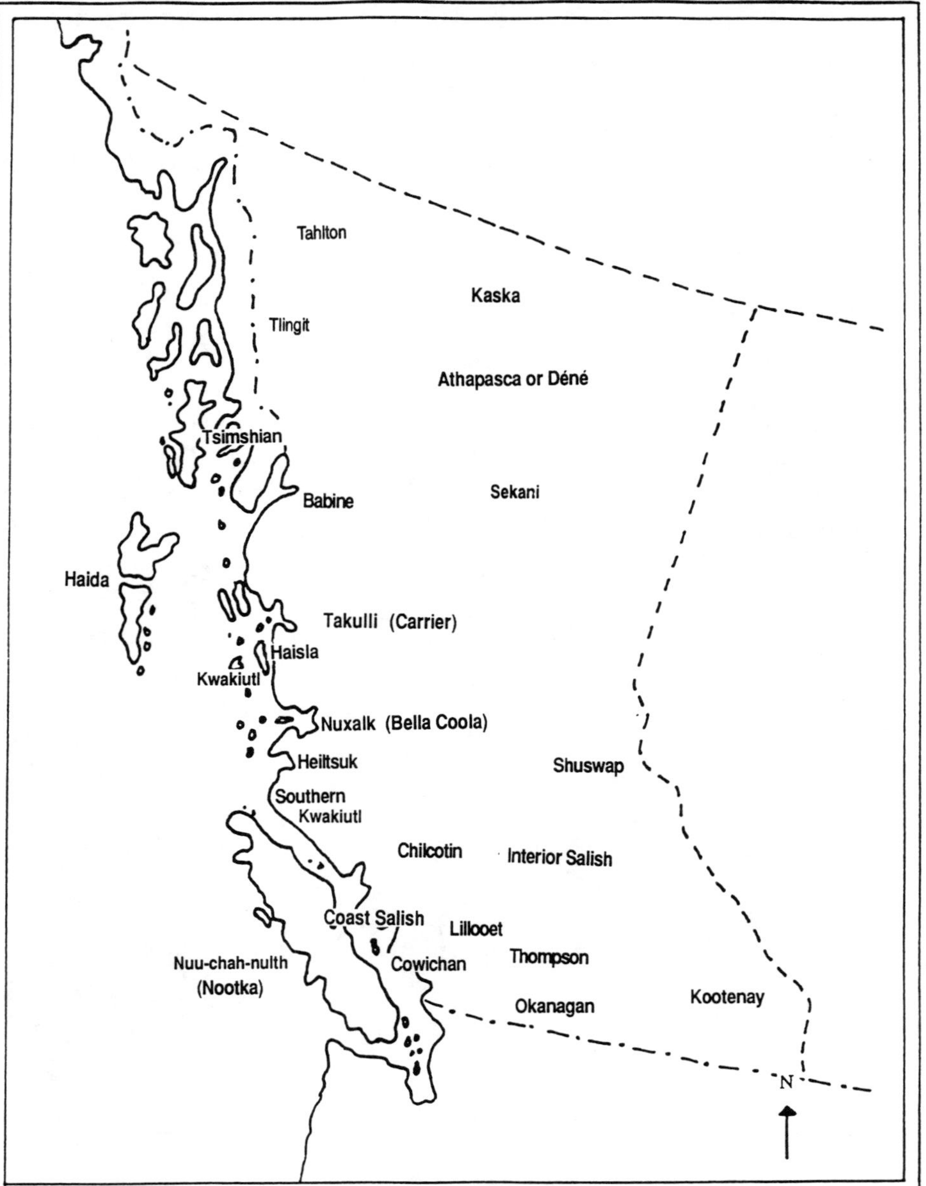

**Native Peoples of
the Northwest Coast**

Native Peoples of the United States

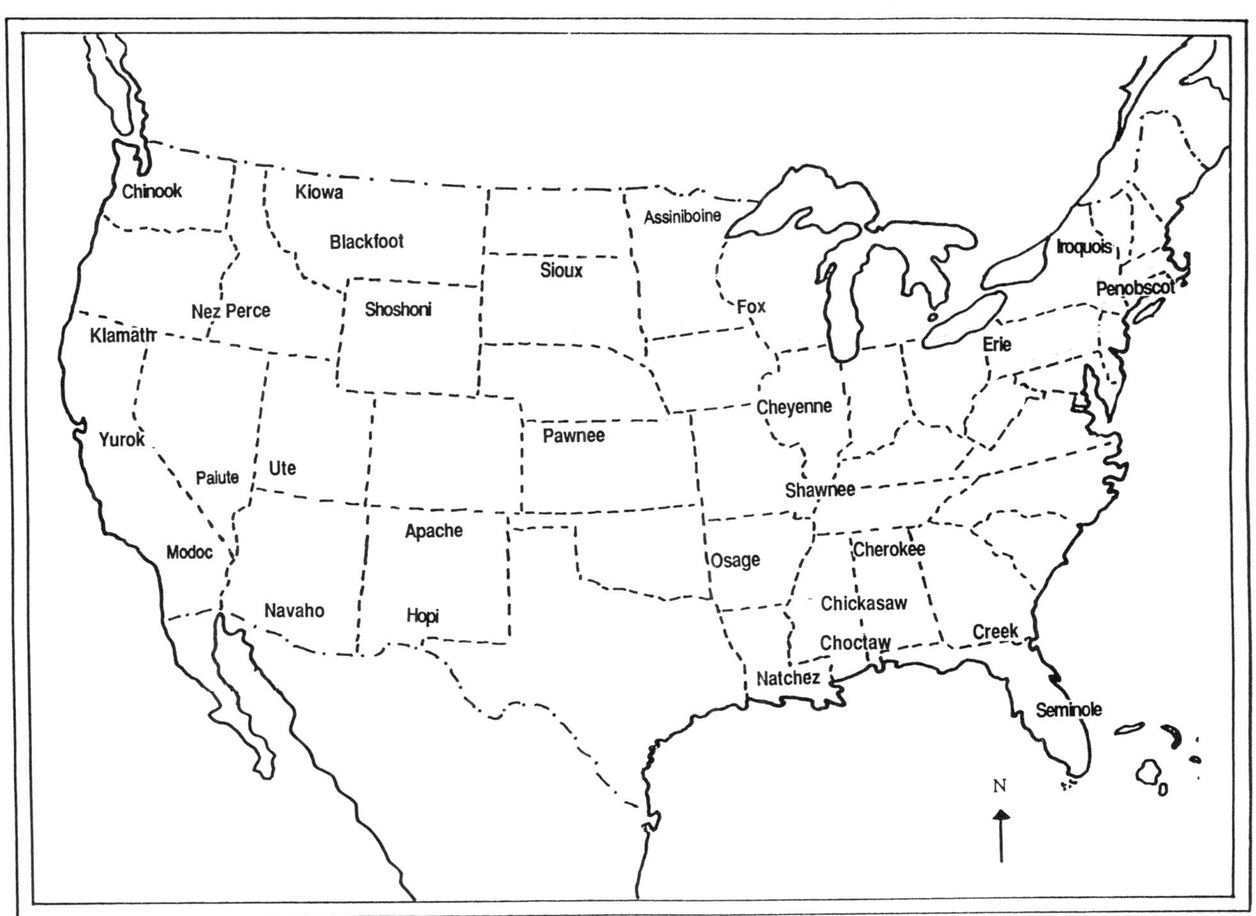